Wingtips with Spurs

Michael L. Gooch, SPHR

First Edition

Multi-Media Publications Inc.
Oshawa, Ontario

Wingtips with Spurs
By Michael L. Gooch, SPHR

Managing Editor: Kevin Aguanno
Copy Editor: Caroline Sori
Typesetting: Charles Sin
Cover Design: Troy O'Brien
eBook Conversion: Agustina Baid

Published by:
Multi-Media Publications Inc.
Box 58043, Rosslynn RPO, Oshawa, Ontario, Canada, L1J 8L6

http://www.mmpubs.com/

ISBN (Paperback):   1-897326-88-2 / 9781897326886
ISBN (Adobe PDF eBook):   1-897326-89-0 / 9781897326893
ISBN (Mobipocket PRC eBook):   1-897326-90-4 / 9781897326909
ISBN (Microsoft LIT eBook):   1-897326-91-2 / 9781897326916
ISBN (Palm PDB eBook):   1-897326-92-0 / 9781897326923

Published in Canada. Printed simultaneously in U.S.A. and England.

CIP Data available from the publisher.

Contents

Dedication 7

Acknowledgements 9

Note to Reader 11

Introduction 13

Absenteeism 17

After Hours 23

Age Discrimination 27

Arguing 33

Bad News 39

Big Picture 43

Communication 47

Conflict 53

Consultants 57

Creativity 63

Decisions 67

Disabilities **71**

Ethics **75**

Fads... No Thanks **81**

Firing **87**

Fun at Work **95**

Government **99**

Hiring **105**

Labor Relations **113**

Leadership **121**

Meetings **129**

Mission Statements **135**

Money **139**

Organizational Charts **143**

Pride **149**

Racial Discrimination **157**

Run (When to) **169**

Safety **175**

Self-Importance **181**

Sexual Harassment 187

Spiritually Connected 191

Standing Plans 209

Strategic Planning 213

Stress 219

Succession 227

Teamwork 233

Training 239

Turnover 247

Value 253

Words 259

Wrap Up 263

Cowboy Wisdom 267

Sacred Words 271

Suggested Reading 277

About the Author 279

Dedication

In Memory

Alton Lee Gooch
1931 – 2005

Acknowledgements

This book was not written by me as much as I was the scribe and recorder of the inspiring and instructional events within my lifetime. As I traveled this road, I often heard people complaining about the horrible boss they were stuck with. In this regard, I have always been extraordinarily blessed. Not that I have not encountered the occasional troll but as an overall experience, I have had many wonderful and inspiring leaders. From each of them, I learned an extremely valuable lesson. I would be remiss not to acknowledge them in a book that, at its core, is really more about them than me.

Many thanks to Jim Zydzik for teaching me the value of high standards and for developing in me a sense of urgency; and to Chuck Piechocki, who helped me understand that a day spent fishing is just as valuable as a day at work. Many thanks to Don Bragdon, who taught me that a true leader must leave their office at times and get in the foxhole. Tom Hill was instrumental in the early days by convincing me that a simple farm boy could really contribute to an organization with something other than a strong back. Art Jones inspired me to operate without fear. a lesson I carry every day and in every way. My gratitude goes to Hank Jacob who provided great support and gave me my first opportunity to move into human resources. Joe Adrian taught me the lesson of thinking through the enemy's defenses. Among a great many other things, Ken Knowles showed me that perseverance is one of our greatest assets. I am grateful to Terry Barnhill for teaching me that the devil is in the details and for overlooking the days when I did something incredibly stupid. Gary Davis inspired me with his spiritual strength and his burning desire to place his spiritual life before everything else.

As I have always possessed the unhealthy trait of acting first and thinking later, I must acknowledge the two attorneys that spent part of their career pulling me out of the mouth of disaster. the late William "Bill" Peterson of Marshall Missouri and Bill Walmsley of Batesville, Arkansas. Unbeknownst to them, I learned valuable lessons in employment law and human nature each time they fixed my mistakes.

I am very thankful to Susan 'Sam' Mason and Laura Lawson for their encouragement to publish this book. My dear friend Sandra Millsap gave me her undying support throughout this process and would often pull me out of the doldrums with her wit and wisdom.

An acknowledgement list would be woefully incomplete without mentioning my supportive family. I am blessed with five very smart and very beautiful children, Vicki, Cathy, Lisa, Jeremiah and Ginger. I thank my mother, Mary Ann, not only for giving me life but for always providing a continuous wellspring of unconditional love. How truly blessed I have been to have been raised by such a remarkable woman. And finally, my reality, my wife, Janita "Bird". Why you chose me to accompany you on this journey through life I will never know. But I'm sure glad you did.

Note to Reader

The author is donating fifty percent of the net proceeds from this book to the St. Jude Children's Research Hospital in Memphis, Tennessee. St. Jude Children's Research Hospital is working hard to find cures and save children everywhere who are fighting cancer and other catastrophic diseases.

If the reader would like to assist St. Jude's in this mission, please donate by calling 1-800-822-6344, or email them at donors@stjude.org. You can also contact them by regular mail at St. Jude Children's Research Hospital, 501 St. Jude Place, Memphis, TN 38105.

Introduction

Welcome to our guide to people management. Whether you are a neophyte or grizzled veteran, you are engaged in a sacred profession. We are the first and last persons an employee sees as they walk in the door and out the door; and so our conduct can change a person forever.

I developed this book with the managerial professional in mind. However, the philosophy and the values contained within are of value to anyone who works with people in reaching organizational goals.

This book is not a detailed discussion of any subject matter. For that, you would need to look elsewhere. You will also not find legal guidance, although the contents will tend to keep you out of court. Finally, you will not be reading a how-to book. If anyone ever writes a veritable management how-to book, I will be the first in line to buy it. The field is too broad and complex to lend itself to a series of action or systematic organization. I firmly believe that the practice of people management is much more art than science. What you will find are suggestions that will develop your philosophy in people management or management in general.

I have spent a good part of my life on the ranch. The years away from it, I often wished I were back. As we built fences, worked cattle, hauled hay, and fought the weather, I often found myself thinking about my other job as a professional manager. I wished that my business career could be as simple as my ranch life. I finally came to the healthy conclusion that they are no different. The principles and lessons from the ranch easily adapt to the corporate world.

The inept rancher and the struggling manager often find they are engaged in a reactionary activity: by failing to plan, failing to maintain core values, and failing to connect to other people, the inept rancher and struggling manager both find themselves constantly having to respond to crises and near disasters. Taken as a Unified Whole, the lessons in this book will assist the struggling manager with leaving behind the reactionary category and becoming a better manager. For those managers who are not fighting for survival, these lessons will help to remind them of the true reason behind our choice of career.

While not all of the advice stems directly from the ranch, all of it is the cowboy way of thinking. I would be foolish to believe that you will agree with all of the suggestions I offer. In fact, I practically guarantee that you will not agree with all of this advice. Whether you agree or disagree, I hope that this book will expand your views and trigger creative thought. My goal was to create a holistic approach to the management of people. While each chapter stands on its own, the totality of *Wingtips with Spurs* will present a philosophical understanding of our goal. I hope that the sum of this book is greater than its individual components and that a 'system' of sorts will arise. The different ingredients in my wife's chili are wonderful when eaten alone. Nevertheless, once she combines them and lets the pot simmer awhile, magic happens.

I sincerely hope you enjoy the book. If you can take away just one small thing, I will have accomplished my goal.

Wingtips with Spurs

1

Absenteeism

"A wise youth harvests in the summer, but one who sleeps during harvest is a disgrace."
Proverbs 10:5

"Nobody ever drowned in his own sweat."
Cowboy Wisdom

Why do we have an absentee problem? When I was a young man, it was unheard of for someone not to show up for work. There were fences to mend, cow to be milked, chickens to be watered and fed. If someone missed his assignment, it was because he was dead or dying! I have seen my father, who would sometimes "get down in his back," work all day and most of the night and then limp out at midnight in a snowstorm to pull a calf during a difficult birth.

What has happened to the work ethic? The further we get from the Great Depression, the worse the attendance problem becomes. Maybe it was the Me Generation which started the spiral. Sometime back, we started a disturbing trend in the nation whereby parents began to focus life around the wants (not needs) of the child; and by now this trend is fully entrenched. I call this the Cult of the Child, and I believe it is a cause of absenteeism and our lack of work ethic in general. Spoiling children, allowing them to back talk, and generally running our adult lives to pacify the child are simply wrong. It is our job to be parents, not accomplices. Not all kids are bad. In fact, most of our younger generation will work and work hard; but the trend does exist, and it is getting away from us. It breeds a spoiled brat who will not work and crumbles under pressure. Even the best of this lot often lacks workplace skills. These poor pampered kids grew up under coddled, permissive conditions where they were told, "No. You're not going to do that and that's kind of, sort of final."

Another national trend that affects the work ethic of our workforce is the drastic escalation in the number of unwed mothers. Nationwide, more than thirty-five percent of women have children without the stability of marriage. For black women alone, the rate is even higher, an estimated seventy percent. Kids raised without steady fathers are twice as likely to drop out of school or become teenage parents. In addition, these kids are one-and-a-half times more likely to be unemployed.

The number of unwed mothers was relatively small before the 1960s. After President Johnson created the Great Society programs, however, the number of out-of-wedlock babies exploded. While the shocking increase in absentee fathers has many roots, I challenge anyone to look at a chart of the national number of unwed mothers over the past fifty years and tell me differently when the problem started.

I don't care what certain segments of society claim: a fatherless child tends to grow up undisciplined and lazy. When this young person shadows your doorway, he or she becomes your personal problem as well as society's. Before you start screaming about the virtues of single motherhood, I fully understand that there are exceptions to the rule. I know that single parents have raised many industrious, intelligent, contributing people. I have a great deal of respect not only for the child who grew into a productive adult in spite of the hardships but also for the parent who succeeded in this most important of endeavors. With that said, these exceptional people are not the norm.

I would have stayed in bed until nine or ten most mornings if my dad had not rolled me out. I was not afraid of my mother; Mama was an easier sale than my dad was. She would listen to my lies about the ache in my side, but Dad did not buy into my attempts at hypochondria and when he said, "frog," I tended to jump. It was amazing how fast I would miraculously heal once Dad got after me. My mother's style of management did not fit the age and attitude of her charge, but Dad's style was clearly understood.

While we cannot repair society, we can change our management style to fit. It boils down to a twofold problem: a young workforce that exhibits the results of having received either too *little* attention as a child or too *much* attention as a child. I realize this is simplistic thinking, but to solve a problem we need to distill it down to its fundamental nature.

Youngsters today are smarter than we ever were. They have a higher intelligence, and so they become bored swiftly. The ones who were given too much attention when they grew up must always be shoveled a liberal dose of praise on a daily basis. If you are not willing to do this because it takes too much time and effort, then you had better learn to live with an absentee rate of three percent or more.

Another 'too much attention' attribute is their reaction to the way we correct their work. If we use phrases such as "speed it up, you're too slow" or "we need better from you," you can expect to hear a whooshing sound as the door shuts behind them. Because the society in which they grew up gives everyone a trophy, they have come to always expect one. With this generation, you have to ease into criticism, so choose your attitude and words carefully. Sure, it takes more time, but you will not spend your time finding and training replacements. Let's also not forget that smart people need to know why they are doing a certain task and how it fits into the big picture. Often, this makes all the difference.

A rancher needed a corral built. He hired two men to work on the job. He explained the layout of the corral to the first man, and how it would become the best in the area. He did not have the opportunity to explain this to the second man. The first day the temperature was 105 degrees, and the two men spent it splitting cedar rails. In the afternoon, the rancher found the second man sitting under a shade tree, so he asked him how it was going. The man said, "The sun's hot, the ax is dull, and my back is killing me." Then the rancher approached the first man, who was using a sledge and maul to split the logs, and asked if the heat were getting to him. "It's a little warm," the first man said, "but it's no problem. The way I see it, we're building the best corral in the county!" I will just bet the second man missed work the next day.

I won't pretend to know what absentee program or policy you should have. There are a hundred of them, ranging from nothing to twelve-page policy manuals detailing 'no fault' systems. Actually, any program works as well as any other as long as it is reasonable. The two things to guard against are being too flexible and not being flexible enough. Sounds like I am chewing cud on both sides of my mouth? Let me explain.

You must maintain proper parameters and boundaries, and everyone must be intimately aware of these boundaries. Just as on the ranch, you need solid fences. A sound fence lets the cattle know the territory they can wander and where they cannot. Just like cattle, some people will always be trying the fence, looking for a weak spot. Do you know what ranchers do with cattle which continually breach the fence? They sell them or eat them.

At the other extreme, we must also guard against the employer who will not allow his people to get time off for important events or is too 'policy driven.' Of course, managers will often say that if they allow someone to go outside the policy they will lose control. Here is a helpful hint. Someone who says that has already lost control. This also reminds me of an old cowboy saying: "A hound dog will always return to a warm home." That pretty much sums it up.

Many times in the past, I have heard managers proclaim, "This is not a popularity contest." Well, I hate to disappoint them, but it really is. The employee who just called in sick voted you Least Popular. Like it or not, these are contests you need to win, place, or show. Need proof? Rank each supervisor or manager of a specific area by his or her employee absentee rank. Chart their area rates and names on a Pareto chart. When you look at the top twenty percent, you are looking at your ineffective managers. This group has lost the popularity contest and should be sent home or at least made to stand in the corner for a while. You will be doing them a favor. They are probably unhappy in their work and should pursue another career path.

Recently, I hired a young man to help build a barbed wire fence. He worked with me, day and night (we used truck lights) fourteen hours a day. It was hot, heavy work. We drove steel posts, dug postholes, and carried rolls of heavy, sharp, barbed wire through thorns and briars. He had never built a fence or even been on a ranch. As we worked, I complimented him on his fence-building abilities, telling him he was becoming a real cowboy. After two days, I told him I could not use him anymore because I had over-spent the budget on hired help. The next day he showed up to work—free. Said he enjoyed it. I paid him anyway.

Lesson from the Ranch

They'll show up tomorrow if you truly appreciate their efforts today.

After Hours

*"Because we belong to the day, we must live decent lives for all to see.
Don't participate in the darkness of wild parties and drunkenness, or in
sexual promiscuity and immoral living, or in quarreling and jealousy."*
Romans 13:13

*"You're only young once. After that, you need some other
excuse for acting like an idiot."*
Cowboy Wisdom

Years ago, my dad would take me to a nearby small town
that held its weekly cattle auction on Saturdays. The
sale barn was a magical place. I loved the smell of the
cattle, hot dogs, diesel fuel, and new leather. Dad would always
buy something, and it was major fun to drive home anticipat-
ing Mom's response.

One of the auction regulars was a man who raised crossbred cattle. You would usually know he was there, as his odor would override the smells of the barn. I don't believe his rear end ever met the bottom of a tub. While he could afford much better, his clothes were grease-stained and torn. How he managed to keep a five-day stubble, I will never know. He looked like the dogs had been keeping him under the porch. As the auctioneer rambled on, this guy took a whiskey bottle out of his pocket and took slugs throughout the day. I never saw him drunk; just never saw him sober. The quality of his cattle was good, but he always failed to achieve even the average auction price. This happened month after month, year after year. Thus, it was obvious that his appearance, behavior, and judgment cast a poor light on his stock.

The same principle holds true for management. More times than I care to count, people say that their off-work behavior doesn't affect the person's job. "(Insert employer name) can't tell me what to do when I get off work. That's my time, not theirs." If you are independently wealthy, stop reading this chapter. If not, may we suggest the following?

Yes, it is your own personal time. However, if someone is in a leadership position, it becomes extremely critical to maintain proper decorum both inside and outside the workplace. Improper decorum can range from getting a DUI to showing up at the grocery store in your flip-flops and no shirt. People look up to a leader, so why disappoint them? Don't get me wrong. I have nothing against a cold beer. I just tend to drink mine while I'm on the ranch and not at the local bar.

In general, partying and socializing with those you supervise is dancing on a landmine. I am not talking about company events or playing cards with your peers. The danger zone is drinking, dancing, and otherwise socializing after hours with people who report to you. If you, as a manager, have someone in a leadership position who is socializing after hours with his or her workers, give your leader one chance to stop. If he or she refuses, it's time to terminate that person. If you find he or she is engaged sexually with a worker, you should terminate the leader immediately. Remember the fence in chapter 1? It's time to sell the cow.

I realize the above advice goes against the modern grain of loose decorum and even looser morals. Nevertheless, could not following such advice be the reason employees file more lawsuits, are less productive, and are constantly updating their résumés? In general, have employees lost respect for management? You decide.

Now that we have taken away all the fun stuff to do after work, what's left? Consider what many refer to as the tripod of health: mental, emotional, and spiritual well-being. Every opportunity we have to work with people, we should be checking on these three areas. How can we manage people if we don't analyze the tripod?

Do they read? What do they read? Do they exercise the brain after work? On the other hand, maybe they take root in front of the television or computer and watch the pretty colors on the screen. Consider suggesting reading material. Better yet, buy them a book that you have enjoyed.

One quick way to check for emotional well-being is to watch the employee's weight. People under too much stress or emotional imbalance will put on weight. The accounting clerk who weighed one hundred and ten pounds in July and weighs one hundred and forty pounds in October usually has issues in the background. Our role is to recognize and help such employees with any hurdles at work or time off needed. Our role is to 'question around the edges' and direct employees to professional assistance.

One thing that has always amazed me is the way many people fall into the 'I worked (insert number) hours' mode. This is especially true of salaried workers. People will walk up and down the corridors spouting off the number of hours they have worked during the day or during the week, wearing the number as a badge of honor. Pardon my bluntness, but I consider it a badge of stupidity. Most of the people you see slinging around their number of worked hours are those who are most in fear of losing their jobs. Alternatively, they are trying hard to impress the boss and therefore earn points. If this kind of thing impresses your boss, you need to find a new one. (The sad thing is that these people rarely actually work. They sit around shooting the bull while taking away from family time.) We would be much happier if our people gave us a productive eight hours and then went home. To break this habit, I have insisted on occasion that a person go home. I know that when a true crisis erupts, they will be well balanced and able to work all the hours we need to resolve the issues. I have worked twenty-four hours a day during union problems or plant emergencies such as fires and floods. I've also knocked off at noon to go fishing. Hanging around work after you are finished just to rack up hours is like riding a rocking horse. It might look impressive, but it gets you nowhere.

Lesson from the Ranch

The strength of a horse is in his bloodline; of a man in his behavior.

Age Discrimination

"And now, in my old age, don't set me aside.
Don't abandon me when my strength is failing."
Psalm 71:9

"When a cowboy is too old to set a bad example,
he hands out good advice."
Cowboy Wisdom

An old gunfighter way past his prime was having a drink in the saloon. A young whippersnapper looking to make his bones called the old fighter out into the street. The old man grimaced as he downed the last gulp and slowly rose, favoring his bad leg. He limped into the dirt causeway. The young man, in an effort to intimidate and impress, drew his pistol at lightning speed and accurately threw two shots at a swinging lantern fifty yards away. Pleased with himself, he re-holstered the pistol and squared off against the old man. The old man showed no emotion but cast a reptilian stare at the young man as the long seconds ticked by. Suddenly, with dazzling speed, the youngster drew and fired. He missed. The old man slowly withdrew his notched pistol, took slow aim, and shot the gun from the boy's hand. Then he strolled up to the young fighter. Looking past him as if watching a parade in the background, the old man said, "You've learned to control your gun, son, but I can tell you'll never be able to control your mind." That said, the old gunfighter rode off. The young wannabe returned to his farm, where his distraught wife and young daughter warmly welcomed him.

I am certain that I wouldn't want to discriminate against the old man in this story. Go ahead and call him out into the street if you want to.

Is our true worth only in what we can physically do, or does it live in the compassion of the heart and the wisdom of the mind?

In 1967 Congress passed a law protecting everyone age forty or over from discrimination on the job. Why in heaven's name they chose forty is beyond me, but forty it is. Nevertheless, if you spend enough time in management you will have to deal with this issue. You may be surprised to discover that the ones filing age-related charges usually belong to the professional and managerial classes. They have college degrees. Their compensation is higher than most. They will fight the company longer and harder. The issuance of a *Right to Sue* letter from the EEOC means just that to them.

In my heart, I don't believe that any management professionals willingly engage in age discrimination. I believe we stumble into it as we go about our day-to-day business. We tend to think of age discrimination in terms of new hires, but forget that it also includes promotions and demotions. I think we are at our most vulnerable when we are in a rush mode to carry out the company's directive to downsize. Keep adverse impact forefront in your mind at all times. Unfortunately, many top managers use downsizing as an opportunity to clean house. If you find yourself in the position of evaluating people instead of how they complete their tasks, clearly state your position. Offer your resignation if the lights don't come on. You don't need to work for this company anyway. Your values and their values are poles apart.

Sometimes, the inappropriate behavior and off-hand remarks of others will sneak up to bite you. Have you ever been blindsided by disparaging remarks made by your management team? They probably don't realize at the time that they are in a discrimination mode. Usually they will 'get it' when their depositions start. When you hear the following phrases, stop the offender, offer some education, and hope to goodness no one else heard them. If it happens again with the same person, it may be time to sell the cow. The courts and juries will decide if the remarks are 'stray comments' or direct evidence of a discrimination mindset.

- "We need sharp, young people."

- "We need people who can come in early and stay late."

- "They're dinosaurs."

- "They're too old to learn something new"

- "We want employees who are young, lean, and mean."

- "They wouldn't be able to keep up with the fast company growth."

- "We're looking for longevity."

- "We need some young blood in this department."

If a manager allows a culture that tolerates remarks such as the ones above, then the manager will probably get what he or she is asking for. The great leader will remind management on a frequent basis that they should never forget silence is often the best answer.

As I stated in chapter 1, our young generation—as a general rule—is smarter than we were. However, do you value knowledge over wisdom? I define knowledge as knowing that I am about to enter a one-way street. I define wisdom as still looking both ways.

You will hear some people claim that older workers have higher absentee rates due to health issues. I think that if you look at the statistics, you will find that older workers take off for longer periods but actually miss fewer days than the forty-and-younger crowd.

Through the years, I have seen older workers singled out to receive severance packages, fail to obtain promotions, or even not being hired to begin with. Sometimes these results were conscious and sometimes, I suspect, subconscious, but each time somebody did not get an opportunity simply because he or she has survived in the workplace longer than others.

Give this test to your managers when they lean toward the younger versus the older: "You are on an airplane at 37,000 feet when the plane is seriously disabled and must make an emergency landing. The oxygen masks drop, and you immediately don yours and then assume the crash position. The next part is totally up to you. You get to decide. Do you want the captain to be young and bushy-tailed, have an advanced degree and be full of energy and excitement, or would you prefer the bored, silver-haired, twenty-year veteran with the prostate problem?" When it concerns my life, I'll take wisdom, knowledge and experience over zeal and a healthy prostate any day.

We will leave this chapter with the following story. An old bull and a young bull were standing on a hill overlooking the herd. The young bull said, "Let's run down and mate with one of those cows." The old bull said, "Let's *walk* down and mate with all of them." The wiser of the two was teaching a life lesson. Even though the older, less-energetic bull recommended a strategy change, this new course offered a richer reward. My wife said I should not include this story in the book. Well, see the second quote in the next chapter.

Lesson from the Ranch

With age comes wisdom and knowledge and their value is incalculable.

4

Arguing

"Don't pick a fight without reason, when no one has done you harm."
Proverbs 3:30

"There are two theories to arguin' with a woman. Neither one works."
Cowboy Wisdom

The word 'argue' has negative connotations. We tend to think it means that emotions are flaring, voices are rising, and we are butting heads. The word doesn't mean that at all. Arguing is the art of disagreeing without being disagreeable. When we argue, we are simply trying to get something we want, even if it is as simple as getting our point across, while the other person is trying to keep us from it. A wise person will make sure that everyone gets what he wants or can live peacefully with the results. Arguing is a two-person dance. If both sides argue, we will achieve consensus or at least be able to live with the decision, but troubles arise when only side argues. In the *Gentle Art of Making Enemies*, James Whistler stated, "I'm not arguing with you—I am telling you." Whistler had obviously discovered a shortcut in making an enemy. When performed correctly, arguing does not create enemies. You create an enemy through arguing only when you do not allow input and some form of consideration.

You might wonder how much arguing can take place on a ranch. Let me assure everyone that not a single day goes by without argument. It is the best way to achieve goals, and when done correctly, everyone is happy. My son, Jeremiah, and I recently argued over the design of a new corral. I wanted to build it in square, straight lines to save cost and—as I argued—to have more corner strength. Jeremiah wanted a corral built on a curved design. In the end, we both got what we were after. The holding pens are square, and the working and loading chutes curve. In the end, our corral is much better than either of our single designs. Thank goodness for arguments.

If you are in the management profession, arguing is a large part of your profession. You may not realize it, but you argue everyday. You argue over important items, such as union contracts, pay rates, benefits, hiring and firing decisions. You also argue over not-so-important items, such as room temperature, coffee brand, parking spaces, office supplies. You may even argue about a raise, a promotion, or the need to relocate.

In the management profession, we should be arguing every day. Frankly, to be successful in the long haul, we will need to win most of these arguments. If managers don't argue, then someone else is calling the important shots without hindrance. If they are having no impact, maybe the company doesn't need them. If they keep arguing but tend to lose, tell me again why we need them?

You may work with brilliant people and be intimated by their intelligence. You may even be a little in awe of their credentials. Don't be sheepish about engaging them in an argument. Remember that they don't have the life experiences that you do. They have not struggled with the things you have. You are a unique individual who brings a lifetime of trials to any argument. Chances are also good that you will know more about the subject matter than they will. The English playwright William Congreve, known for his comedies, summed up our behavior of agreeing with the intelligentsia when he said, "I am always of the opinion of the learned, if they speak first."

The people who report to you and those to whom you report should argue with you every day. It keeps everyone honest and allows the best ideas to flow. A manager should have no prouder moment than when his or her subordinate wins an argument. It shows that the manager has developed a culture that openly encourages freethinking, and besides, the manager now has a subordinate who has achieved job satisfaction, self-esteem, and loyalty. If the manager really does his or her job right, someday the manager could be reporting to the subordinate. No greater compliment could be handed to a manager.

Arguing is not assaulting the other person. Arguing is not slinging insults and getting in someone's face. Arguing should be about passion, but always keep a tight lid on your emotions. Look at the careers and marriages that have been destroyed because emotions ran unchecked and words were used as weapons. Remember, rudeness and ignorance attend the same family reunion.

Back in the 1960s, there was a traveling tent preacher by the name of Harvey Starling. Mom and Dad would drag me to these sawdust revivals every year to see Brother Starling rain hellfire and brimstone down on the crowd. I'll admit I didn't care much for him. If I am going to a tent, I want to see elephants and the highflying trapeze, and all I got was some crazy-eyed person scaring me. However, one thing the preacher said stuck with me through the years. He claimed that he and his wife never argued. No sir, they never argued, not once. As the assembled leaned forward, you could tell they wanted to hear the deep secret this man of God was about to bestow. Brother Starling continued, "We've never argued, but you can often hear us reasoning things out about a mile away." Well, so much for deep secrets.

Sometimes you can argue too much. I am guilty of this (see the Bible verse that begins this chapter). I sometimes argue just for the sake of the contest. I especially like to see how the other person constructs his argument. Does he or she use passion? How important is this issue and why? I must confess that sometimes I'll take an opposing view that I don't agree with just for the chance to joust. I practice my arguing so that my sword will be sharp for the important battles ahead.

Now, all of the above sounds warm and fuzzy, but how do we win arguments? I can't tell you how to win your arguments because arguments come from within. They are personal. Each person's argument will be as unique as a snowflake. I can only tell you what works for me.

1. *Be passionate about the subject.* If you're not willing to invest emotional energy, why should the other person(s) even pretend to grant you what you want? Passion is the key to a full life. It is important in our chosen fields, our pastimes, the arts, music, our love lives. It is important in how we argue. You care enough about the matter to invest the time and energy of at least two people. Thus, we should care enough about it to invest passion.

2. *Explain your position while checking for understanding.* Then, let the other person have the power to decide. That's right: give the other person all of the power. It is amazing how well this works. Most of the time, the other person will decide on your side. You leave with what you wanted, and the other person knows the choice—and the

power—was totally in his or her hands. You will find other material that states just the opposite. They will claim that you should never concede any power to the other person. I wonder how many arguments they have actually won. I know how many I have.

3. *Learn to be a compromising person.* How simple this concept is, yet how often it is not used. Both sides can claim victory. Both sides get what they wanted—albeit not the whole enchilada. If our egos are so large that we cannot compromise, then we should find another line of work. Maybe there is a tollbooth hiring where you can demand the exact change, or else.

4. *Realize that you are not going to win every time and probably should not.* Sometimes you will just need to stop arguing and do as you are told, especially in situations involving your boss or spouse. As they say in Wyoming, "Time to paint your butt white and run with the antelope."

As a final point, I cannot end this chapter without talking about arguing with myself. The downside is that both sides are passionate. The upside is that I cannot lose.

Lesson from the Ranch

Embrace the person that argues. Be fearful of those who don't.

Bad News

"Someone once told me, 'Saul is dead,' thinking he was bringing me good news. But I seized him and killed him at Ziklag. That's the reward I gave him for his news!"
2 Samuel 4:10

"Unlike bad weather, bad news doesn't get better over the next few days."
Cowboy Wisdom

anching is a natural draw for bad news: mad cow disease, falling cattle prices, rising grain prices, drought, equipment breakdowns, rustlers (yes, they still exist). Even if the news is not bad, the typical rancher will twist it until it looks bad. Like ranching, American industry is flooded with bad news. It is just a natural part of life. How we handle bad news is a direct reflection of our leadership and sets us apart from the crowd. How we communicate bad news to our staff will determine if we are successful or if we need to start stuffing envelopes.

The true leader will receive bad news, digest its meaning personally, and then concentrate on how it might negatively affect the employees. The next step is to leap into a positive zone. Is this solely bad news, or could some good news come out of it? How many people are really affected? Has this bad news been anticipated by the rumormill? If so, the bad news itself is often not as bad as the rumors have painted it.

It is most important to remain calm. The worse the news, the calmer a leader will become. As the team goes into crisis overdrive, they will look for the calm center. Our behavior during times of bad news will determine if we stay focused or dive into chaos. Our appropriate conduct will solidify our leadership position, and we will come out of the fire stronger and sharper than ever before. All we have to do is remain calm and deliver the news. Someone once noted that Ulysses S. Grant "doesn't scare worth a damn." That pretty much sums it up.

Many leaders avoid delivering bad news at any cost. William Shakespeare wrote, "Though to be honest, it is never good to bring bad news; give to a gracious message a host of tongues, but let ill tidings tell themselves when they be felt." How we convey bad news is as important as our personal conduct in receiving the bad news. The way the bad news is delivered will have a short-term impact and often long-term consequences. Never use emails or memos to deliver bad news; or delegate this responsibility. Bad news should always be delivered in person.

We should not look to soften the impact. Now is not the time for being mealy-mouthed. People need straight talk. Don't try to protect people from the truth, but explain the situation as clearly as possible. If you were in some way responsible for the bad news, 'fess up immediately and be done with it. People will want to ask hard questions, so be prepared to wrap up with a Q&A. Delivering bad news is a tough business; which is why it's up to the leader to complete this task. "

However, if there is a positive aspect, it should definitely be included in your talks. Nature teaches us that, like sunshine after a storm, bad news should always be followed by good news. This should be a new rule you implement in your life. Look hard, look deep, and look often over the next couple of days to find good news and share it with everyone. Good news brings joy to the workplace. Good news generates good thoughts and feelings, which in a variety of wonderful ways. Suddenly, the entire organization is feeling creative and supportive. Bickering and complaining cease. As a pleasant surprise, bad news rarely if ever follows. All of this simply by following one simple rule:

Lesson from the Ranch

Handle bad news like an attacking grizzly. Recognize it. Kill it quickly. Then have bear meat for dinner.

Wingtips with Spurs

Big Picture

"But my life is worth nothing to me unless I use it for finishing the work
assigned me by the Lord Jesus."
Acts 20:24

"Boots, chaps, and cowboy hats ... nothing else matters."
Cowboy Wisdom

My ranch is a family operation: my son Jeremiah, son-in-law Josh, and the occasional hired hand (old term but still in use on farms and ranches) provide most of the manual labor. They also provide great ideas for improvement. Nine times out of ten, if the budget allows, we'll go forward with their ideas and suggestions. However, that tenth time I will say no. Like it or not, I have the Big Picture role. If the suggestion doesn't fit into the overall goal, I don't allow the expenditure.

Imagine you are in a helicopter looking over the 'situation.' At ten thousand feet, you can see the entire area and most of the surrounding landscape. At this level, you see the topography, the streams, fauna, and any population centers. This view allows you to tie it all together; but one thing you can't see are the details. No matter how hard you squint, the details remain blurry. That is the reason successful managers should leave the details to others on the ground. I don't buy into the working manager theory that the manager works on the ground with everyone else. Don't take this too literally. I work just as hard as anyone else does. Even so, from a mental perceptive, I remain at ten thousand feet. If you have supervisors and managers who tend to stay on the ground, push them into the helicopter. That's the only way they can do their jobs properly.

Years ago, I worked with a senior vice president who decided that all managers would become 'working managers,' particularly in the support areas. In short order, he had us eliminate most of our supervisory staff and all of our clerical assistants. This swiftly moved the remaining staff and me into the highest-paid clerical pool in the state. Rather than managing, we spent our days huddled over our desks performing the clerical duties that were essential to our operations. I'm not sure if the vice president had a moment of clarity or was smacked in the head by a rock, but he finally came to his senses and allowed us to fill the old positions.

In a large organization, you will have several helicopters and planes in the area. The first-line leaders will be up on metaphorical ladders enhancing their view. You will be at ten thousand feet. Your boss will be cruising above you at twenty thousand feet, able to see more of the landscape than you can. In this way your boss will be able to warn you of impending disasters headed your way and help keep you on course. However, they will be able to see fewer details than you can.

Taking this analogy to the limits, remember that the higher you go, the less oxygen to the brain. This could explain some of my past mistakes.

My wife, Janita, is the accounting manager for the ranch. This is an unpaid and under-appreciated position. She juggles our savings accounts, checking accounts, and credit cards. She does a fantastic job keeping everything solvent. Janita has the final call on whether we spend money or not. I never question her because this is one of the details and is completely her responsibility. At the same time, I decide the Big Picture map. I make the call on the overall growth, expansion, or modifications of the ranch. Occasionally, she will attempt to explain the decisions about the purse strings. At this point, my eyes glaze over. It's not that I don't care. Indeed, I care deeply. It is only that these details are not my job. If I get involved in details, I will lose my perspective.

A critical aspect of your leadership role is to ensure that the detail people are competent and have the organization's interest at heart. Then back off and let them do their work. Your main job is to listen to their advice and believe in it.

Lesson from the Ranch

A hawk sees the big picture. The mouse doesn't. Questions?

CHAPTER

7

Communication

"Wise words satisfy like a good meal; the right words bring satisfaction."
Proverbs 18:20

"Never miss a good chance to shut up."
Cowboy Wisdom

Take a trip back into time, say AD 1550. You could communicate via a few rare books and, if you lived in Europe, a few newspapers. One of the biggest complaints in society was the lack of communication. Spring ahead to AD 1950. Many communication devices have now arisen, such as the television, radio, telegraph, telephone, LP records, postal services, and talking motion pictures. These were all wonderful communication streams and a quantum leap from medieval times; however, communication still remained a major problem. In boardrooms across America, CEOs were shouting that they needed more communication within the organization. Take a short hop to the current day. We now have Blackberries, cellphones, text messaging, blogging, the Internet, teleconferencing, intranet, webcam, email, instant messaging, …. So why do we still have communication failures?

If you work long enough in this old world, you will soon tire of hearing about communication problems. As Strother Martin said, "What we've got here is failure to communicate." Communication takes the heat for everything when plans fail. In eighty percent of the meetings you attend, you will hear communication's name used in vain. In actuality, lack of communication is a symptom of a lack of execution: we either did or did not do something. This usually boils down to one of the following:

1. The sender doesn't know.

2. The receiver doesn't care.

Let us break it down. If the sender 'doesn't know,' this simply means that they are imparting information which is not one hundred percent correct. This happens 24/7 and is really an amazing fact. Take a couple of items from your daily correspondence and really dig deep. You will often find that the information you were given is not correct: maybe not wholly wrong, but somehow, the truth, the whole truth, and nothing but the truth suffered in the exchange. As this incorrect information passes around, people do what they tend to do: they add or subtract to the message. In the end the receiver gets a message which is not the truth but also not a lie, and therefore lies somewhere in the middle. (Although sometimes it is just a blatant lie—see the chapter on ethics.) Sometimes we hide the truth because we invent a correlation between two factors that never existed. As an example, when I was a kid, Dad and Mom would take me to church every Sunday, rain or shine. Toward the end of the services, some crackers would be passed around and each of us would take a tiny bite. Then some little cups of grape juice would be passed around. I was usually hungry by this time of day, but they wouldn't let me have any more. After the crackers and grape juice lunch, dad would put ten dollars in the collection plate. I thought that was an awful lot of money to pay for a little bit of cracker and a sip of grape juice. As an adult, I still have this problem. The correlation that I sometimes imagine exists plainly doesn't, and therefore, the *truth* I tell to others is wrong.

When the receiver 'doesn't care,' communication gets scary. It may be that they simply are not paying attention and are daydreaming about lunch. They care more about the hamburger and fries than about the message you are sending. Here is a short list of reasons why the receiver might fall into the 'doesn't care' category:

1. He or she is disgruntled on the job and could not care less about the message.

2. He or she feels superior to the sender and doesn't really listen.

3. He or she has personal problems at home that distract from the receiver's ability to focus.

4. He or she doesn't consider the subject matter important.

5. He or she has a different view on the matter and isn't open to the message.

6. He or she has racial prejudices that skew the message.

7. He or she dislikes the sender, thereby missing the message.

8. He or she doesn't feel part of the team and disregards the message.

9. He or she is receiving too much information and needs to reboot.

10. He or she is bored stiff with the presentation or sender and has lost all interest. (Let's lower the lights and show this PowerPoint presentation with 75 slides on the capacity analysis of the variables chart with nonconformities.)

11. He or she retired and forgot to tell someone.

I am sure you could add further to this list. One item to consider would be the differences in communicating between the sexes. The biggest difference I see here is that men rudely interrupt conversations so often that women get to the point that they just don't care. That's just the way men communicate. Of course, men interrupt men all the time, and no one seems to care. Women have a different take on this process. They tend to allow others to finish what they are saying before responding. When men interrupt them in mid-sentence, women think this is poor form at best and rude at worse. Men do not mean to be rude, that's just the way they communicate. I would suggest more study on this matter, if you have not done so already.

We now have a situation in which the sender is sending a half-baked message and the receiver doesn't care. No wonder we constantly carp about poor communication. Thus, the advice from the ranch is to make people aware of two simple points: dispense less information, but ensure its accuracy. With this lessened load, there is no excuse not to turn on the brain. Some people, by their nature, just love to hear themselves talk. This greatly waters down their message. It is hard to listen if your eyes glaze over. 2 Maccabees states, "It is a foolish thing to make a long prologue and to be short in the story itself." 2 Maccabees was probably composed in

Greek late during the first century BC, which tends to make me think I am not on the cutting edge of communicative analysis. We ignore the wisdom of our ancestors far too often.

On the ranch, cowboys usually don't talk much. When they do, people around the cowboys listen. There is an old story about two drovers who were at trail's end and had sought lodging in a stable. Before going to sleep, one of the drovers said, "It sure is cold in here." The next morning, he was surprised to see his partner saddling up his horse. The first drover asked if his partner was leaving already. The other drover said, "Yep, you talk too much."

As a last word on communication, I would like to mention that I think we are guilty of communicating too much by email and text messaging. It is very handy, and they are wonderful tools when used properly. Nevertheless, most issues and topics require face-to-face communication. How many times have you seen email spats between two people with everyone and their dogs copied on the messages? This drains energy from the organization and presents a very unprofessional tone. A good manager will put a stop to this nonsense.

I am also concerned about recent articles about employers terminating employees by email. I even read a news story that detailed how an employee was fired by text message. This is not only poor management but is—in my view— morally bankrupt. If I ever do this, you have my permission to shoot me and put me out of my misery.

When we communicate, we need to remember that we may think we know the facts, but often we don't have the whole story. To illustrate: an old cowboy was lying sprawled across two seats in a Dodge City movie theater. The usher approached the cowboy and told him he could use only one seat. The cowboy just rolled his eyes. As this was a Saturday night, the disrespectful cowboy was obviously drunk. The usher, now upset, told the cowboy that he was going to call the police if the cowboy did not cooperate. The usher asked the cowboy his name. The cowboy moaned, "Paul." The usher asked, "Where you come from?" Paul grimaced and said, "The balcony."

Lesson from the Ranch

Figure out quickly whether they don't know or don't care.

Conflict

"Then they began to argue among themselves about who would be the greatest among them."
Luke 22:24

"Speak your mind but ride a fast horse."
Cowboy Wisdom

Thirty-eight years ago, a neighbor's bull was straying on our ranch. While visiting, he sowed his wild oats. I am sure he was having a great time, but we were raising only registered stock so it was a major problem. Of course, the neighbor claimed that the fence belonged to us, and it was our responsibility. So we held a meeting (sitting on a tailgate) to decide the matter once and for all. We came away with an agreement that both sides would pitch in to build a new, sturdier fence. We no longer had a handsome stranger dating our cattle, the neighbor no longer had to search for his bull, and both parties could brag about the new fence.

Conflict on the ranch will usually arise from surrounding landowners or people wanting input on what you do in and around your land. The only way to deal with this is eyeball to eyeball, that is, no emails, no talking to others, no hiding from the dispute. Get it out, have it out, and be done with it. Otherwise, it will fester into a real problem that will cause you to lose sight of your goals. Usually, the one with the most passion wins. As with most things, this is not always bad and can result in improvements or compromises. Conflict at work is no different.

Numerous articles have been written about avoiding or reducing conflict in the workplace. I suspect people with low self-esteem and little confidence wrote these articles. I would also bet the ranch that they usually lose their arguments (see the chapter on arguing).

Embrace conflict as a healthy environment. Conflict shows a passion for the processes, systems, policies, workflow, and, ultimately, the bottom line. If you owned your own company, wouldn't you want passionate people involved?

Conflict is at the heart of life. Pick up any fictional novel, and you'll see that conflict is at the center of the plot. Conflict makes life rich. Never discourage conflict in an organization. What was the last movie you watched? Did it contain conflict? How would the movie have been if you removed the conflict from the script?

Conflict resolution is also important, albeit not as complicated as many think. Resolution is important only from the standpoint that if the conflict goes on too long, it begins to drain and will eventually result in long-term animosity. Most conflict resolves itself in time. However, there will be times when you will need to step in. For me, the best method of resolution is also the oldest method: put both parties in a room by themselves and let them work it out. (You may want to hang around as moderator.) If you have strong feelings about this matter, keep them to yourself; because if you take sides, you'll fail. Even if the parties were physically far apart, I would still manage to get them in a room together. We miss too many communication cues on the telephone.

Looking back over the years, I would estimate this method works at least eighty percent of the time. The other twenty percent of the time, one or both parties leave the organization after having brought everyone's morale down with their disgruntled attitudes. That's why, after an initial failure, it is best to set another meeting the following day or week and take another stab at resolving the matter. Sometimes, like bulldogging a steer, you just have to wear it down.

Lesson from the Ranch

Conflict like water, sustains life. However, like water, take on too much and you drown.

Wingtips with Spurs

Consultants

"Timely advice is lovely, like golden apples in a silver basket."
Proverbs 25:11

"Never ask a barber if he thinks you need a haircut."
Cowboy Wisdom

A wise rancher uses consultants. We have government agencies and universities that will help you with questions about soil conditions, forage nutrition, and animal husbandry in general, at no cost to the rancher. Moreover, the agencies and universities don't pretend to tell us how to run our business. We can accept the advice or not. In addition to the formal groups, we have a network of friends and neighbors always willing to advise if needed. Even ranchers and farmers informally share a tremendous amount of information. We discuss all the latest techniques and technologies at length in the community.

I wish that consulting in the business world would follow this model. Unfortunately, it doesn't. Consulting in the business arena is always used to bolster short-term stock growth. In general, it has two functions:

1. To eliminate people, thereby keeping blood off management's hands.

2. To identify and address incompetent management.

The consultants spend time with your first-line and middle management people, observing and listening. They then take what the first-line and middle managers told them, repackage it in big words, throw in some charts and graphs, and laugh all the way to the bank. Sadly, eighty percent of the time we could have avoided this hugely expensive endeavor if we had only listened to our own people. But then again, what was it Jesus said about being a prophet in your own country?

Another thing to be aware of is the Hawthorne effect, whereby a process improves merely by the act of observation and measurement. While this particular study has been discounted by some, other experiments have validated the underlying theory. Consultants don't like to talk about this effect, but would prefer you to believe that the initial improvements were solely due to their efforts. If I were the consultants, I would not want to discuss the Hawthorne effect either. Suffice it to say, it is a real phenomenon, and one you should be aware exists. A good manager must be able to distinguish between the Hawthorne Effect and the work of Widget Consulting.

More often than not, management professionals find themselves in the "do we need a consultant" loop. When the organization is adamant about moving forward with this process, try to convince them that the smaller firms are the best. The big multinational firms are full of young Turks who are frankly a bit too gleeful about job elimination. Older, wiser people staff the small firms, and. their advice and counsel tend to last after they leave. The young Turks, on the other hand, will restructure your organization in such a way that it will backslide over the next six to eighteen months. Not only have I witnessed the backsliding at organizations where I worked; but where I was intimately involved as a consultant, I noted in my follow-up visits that management had returned to the old processes, forsaking the new and improved. To counter this pattern, I implemented a few lessons in change management before implementing new ideas.

For clarification's sake, I am not opposed to consulting. In fact, I have performed quite a bit of consulting in the past, both as an individual and with a large firm. In certain situations, using a consultation firm makes sense, not to manage the organization for you but rather as a resource that will have the time, tools and people you otherwise wouldn't have. That being said, allow me to paraphrase Mickey Rourke in the movie *Barfly*: "It's not that I don't like consultants. I just feel better when they're not around."

Years ago, I was working with a Fortune 50 company in crisis. Previous CEOs had been operational men progressing to the top, and under their leadership, the company had prospered and grown. The CEO now in charge was an attorney, which seems to be a current trend in America. His answer was to eliminate a quarter of all employees. Thus, a large consulting firm was hired, and they went about their tasks. One of the satellite operations that fell within my scope of responsibility had a history of theft and general malfeasance due to its distance from management. To address this issue, we had bolstered security over the years with twenty-four-hour security coverage.

The most recent security guard we had hired was a retired old man. Years ago, he had been a rancher. Quality of beef and innovation were the hallmarks of his ranch, which had been awarded the County Farmer of the Year Award by the. Farm Bureau . Although it had been a struggle at times, the ranch was successful and provided not only income but, more importantly, pride. However, due to health reasons, he had had to sell out lock, stock, and barrel. As the years went by, he had begun to feel unimportant and unwanted.

Now on the new job, this retired fellow was punctual, honest, professional, and simply loved the work he was doing. Due to his ability to resolve problems and general demeanor, the small workforce respected him. The ranch had given him wisdom. On the rare occasions I saw him on the job, he was always happy-go-lucky and full of advice on ways to improve the job and make life easier for all of us. Sometimes, I took his advice, sometimes I didn't. At home, I was told he bored his wife with stories about his security job and the important role he played in the strategy of the organization. Having felt useless after retirement, this man found that the job gave his life meaning. In return, for roughly $6 an hour, he saved his company unquantifiable amounts of money and equipment from walking out the door.

Having finished with the main operations, the consultants needed a pound of flesh from this small operation. Along with two young consulting Turks, I met with the site manager and the vice president of operations. The Turks recommended that, due to the small scale of this satellite operation, security was not necessary and should be eliminated, thereby giving us three "heads" and saving $43K a year. I sat there in silence. The vice president was not happy with this recommendation but reluctantly agreed. The two Turks stood up from their chairs and actually high-fived each other. Let me rephrase— they high-fived each other in their elation over someone losing a job. With that, they left, and the vice president asked me to deliver the news. The other two guards took it in stride and had other plans in mind. The old man, however, was devastated. From his reaction, you would have thought someone had died. Unlike the younger guards, this was all he had. This job gave him purpose and a reason to get up every day. It was sad watching him turn in his uniforms, radio, and badge. He kept his security coat since these were special ordered. After his termination, he kept this coat hanging in his closet ready for immediate use. He felt like the decision must be a mistake.

Due to a rise in malfeasance, we recalled the two younger guards three months down the road — they were still available — and put them on twelve-hour shifts to avoid the third headcount. We paid dearly in overtime, but at least the organizational chart did not show three blocks.

We never recalled the old man. He never went to work anywhere else. Of course, he kept talking about the job, but over time, he mentioned it less and less. In the end, he battled pancreatic cancer for more than a year. He passed away two years ago and was buried on his old ranch. The coat is still hanging in the closet, ready for the call. You see, the old man was my father. I miss him every day.

Oh, and by the way, the company continued to fail, resulting—finally—in the CEO's removal.

Lesson from the Ranch

Consultants are often hired to fix absent or poor leaders. Understand that they can't polish a cowpile.

CHAPTER
10

Creativity

"It should be explained that all the Athenians as well as the foreigners in Athens seemed to spend all their time discussing the latest ideas."
Acts 17:21

"Never, ever tell a cowboy how to do something. Tell 'em what you need, then watch how resourceful he can be."
Cowboy Wisdom

A successful cow/calf operation is not just the result of planning and hard work. Creativity plays a central role in paying the banker. Unlike standardized industrial processes, each ranch is unique. Challenges and opportunities differ. My soil, water, and topography will be different from yours. My stock will have different genetics even though they may be the same breed. Some ranches operate with an adequate cash flow while others struggle with the simple purchases. A successful rancher cannot simply read a how-to-book or depend exclusively on friendly advice. The rancher must develop new ideas and concepts or combine the old with the new. The rancher who refuses to be creative will wind up working in town.

Many equate creativity with art, music, and literature. This is true, but creativity should run through every aspect of our lives, including the workplace. Indeed, it is a manager's responsibility to encourage creativity in the organization. Not only will greater workplace creativity result in higher profits, but it will also improve employee satisfaction and raise team morale. I am highly concerned that today's culture is not creative. We no longer invent the new. We are good at improving or combining existing technology, but we fail to come up with creative new solutions to problems. The computer has been around since 1945. Oh sure, we have improved and downsized it, but we haven't invented anything to replace it. The combustion engine was a neat invention in its day. Henry Ford found it a useful utilitarian motor. Although it has been improved, it is still the same old concept that resides in your brand-new vehicle. We have satellite dishes, cellphones, and GPS locators—all based on radio waves. There is nothing new here, just alterations of existing products. The latest, greatest invention was supposed to be the Sedgway. Let's see, gyroscopes, batteries, a platform, and wheels? Been there, done that. We have become a nation of windsuckers and stargazers, replacing Benjamin Franklin, Albert Einstein, and Thomas Edison with Donald Trump, video games, and reality TV. We sit behind our desks pushing paper from the left to the right. We don't know how to be creative, only obedient. We have even lost the courage and creative drive to send people into space. Now we send out remote-controlled tricycles (radio waves, computer, camera, and wheels). Science has pushed the envelope in the past decade with the ability—albeit flawed—to produce genetically identical clones. Nature has been doing this for quite a while—without flaws. We call them twins.

Many tools have been used to cultivate a creative workforce. Even as each ranch is unique, each individual organization will have its own special needs, which means you will have to customize to your location. When it comes to creativity, one size does not fit all.

For me, the best approach is to delegate with wide-open parameters and then gently assist the person in finding the solution. Sometimes, the person will fail, but that's okay. The more this happens, the more creative the person becomes, until, finally, you have someone who constantly uses creative thinking. You have someone who enjoys going to work each day. You have someone who feels that he or she is contributing to a greater team effort. You have someone who is loyal. In fact, you may have helped to mold a person who will one day be your boss. That is a great thing, too.

Maybe this approach is not your cup of tea. Nevertheless, quit pushing paper around your desk, and find an approach or system that generates creativity in others. Your employer will thank you. The employee will thank you. Moreover, you will find you have more time to study how you are going to spend your new raise.

Lesson from the Ranch

You were hired for your mind. The mule they bought for the heavy toting.

11

Decisions

"The king speaks with divine wisdom; he must never judge unfairly."
Proverbs 16:10

"The chuck wagon's menu has two selections.
Eat one of them or go hungry."
Cowboy Wisdom

A s in the above cowboy quote, some decisions are easy. Sometimes the decisions come from above, and even though you might strongly disagree, the only recourse is to accept them. We have a saying on the ranch: "Sometimes you got to back up and let the big dogs eat." This sums it up. Still, in the managerial arena, you constantly make decisions. Do I hire this person? Do I fire this person? Do I push this case to the legal system? What salary structure should I use?

What is the decision on this conflict? Do I allow this personal leave? And so on, and so on. Every day, we make decisions, and as they say in physics, the universe splits. Our decisions today determine the picture for tomorrow. Good or bad, we create our own environment by the conclusions we arrive at and the choices we make. Some days, I think the worst decision of the day is deciding to get up.

Decisions have two attributes: weight and time. The weight of the decision asks whether it is tough or easy: what is the overall impact? The vast majority of managers resist making tough decisions. They don't want to be the one to shut down an operation or terminate a long-term employee. Making tough decisions is an integral part of a manager's duties, yet few are truly capable and most will try to delegate or procrastinate, hoping it will go away. Everyone (or 'most everyone) wants to be liked, and most feel that making the tough decisions in life is not a means to this end. However, like a cancer, a tough decision will rarely go away on its own. Instead, it metastasizes and spreads into other areas of the organization.

The cousin to the tough decision is the timely decision. This is a tightrope that few have mastered, but which should be a goal for everyone. One of the most frustrating aspects of middle management is waiting for other people's decisions. Often, no one can move forward without someone from above making a decision, sometimes a tough one, but more often than not an easy decision that shouldn't involve a lot of internal struggle. I find that people put off making decisions on time because they want to avoid conflict or looking stupid. In truth, conflict rarely arises. There is an old saying about people getting out of the way of a man who knows where he is going. If you don't want to look stupid, how do you suppose you look by being indecisive? Even if your decision is wrong, you had the backbone to make it. Now, everyone can move forward.

Making tough, timely decisions is a hallmark of a great leader. is not easy to do, making great leaders a rarity. In 1978, Professor Noam Chomsky said, "As soon as questions of will or decision or reason or choice of action arise, human science is at a loss." Following the professor's logic, this pushes decision making into the arena of art. You can teach decision-making processes, but you can't teach the art of making good decisions.

I have a distant cousin who operates a hog farm. Years ago, he was a representative in the state legislature. While he was serving, the legislators couldn't make a decision about closing a state entity. There were many long-winded debates, with various solutions floated in the air. In the end, the legislators knew that the entity had outlived its usefulness and had to go. As the decision dragged on, the debate, along with the associated state employees, became more and more agitated. One morning, my cousin took the floor and told this story. He said he had heard about a man who was going to bob his dog's tail. When my cousin visited the man and his dog, the floor of the kennel was a bloody mess with one-inch pieces of tail strewn about. My cousin asked the dog owner what was going on. The dog owner said he thought it would be easier on the dog to cut off an inch a day instead of cutting off the whole tail at once. I understand the representatives made the final decision and liquidated the entity that afternoon.

Lesson from the Ranch

Don't cut off an inch of tail a day. Be the decision-maker who can make the timely, tough calls.

CHAPTER 12

Disabilities

"You have not taken care of the weak. You have not tended the sick or bound up the injured. You have not gone looking for those who have wandered away and are lost. Instead, you have ruled them with harshness and cruelty."
Ezekiel 34:4

"Life ain't about how fast you run or how high you climb, but how well you bounce."
Cowboy Wisdom

During my teenage years, I had a good friend named Billy. He was a pleasant, easygoing person. Like me, he threw the shot put and ran track. He was faster than I was and could throw further, but without my style and grace. He couldn't beat me in the bench press, but he came close. We also played football together. He was an offensive lineman, and I was a running back. I simply had to run through the holes he blasted. As I recall, he made the All-District team in his senior year. Billy was not any different from my other friends except that he was born without a right arm. To outsiders, Billy appeared disabled, but I sure wouldn't want to be the one to tell him that. That would have been a quick route to a good, ole-fashioned whupping.

Apparently, the politicians had never heard of Billy; so they enacted the Americans with Disabilities Act of 1990 (ADA). The ADA created quite a stir when it became law. Every manager in the nation was scampering around looking for ways to comply while swearing the sky was falling. Consultants got rich in a hurry by handing out nebulous advice.

As it turns out, the ADA didn't change the business world one iota except for the installation of seldom-used ramps. We see the occasional EEOC/ADA claim, but they are usually bogus. It is a rare occasion when someone who is truly disabled is, in fact, discriminated against. The truth of the matter is that most managers complied with the spirit of the law well before it was passed. In fact, I can't recall a single manager I have known who wouldn't at least try to provide 'reasonable accommodations' for someone with a disability. Still, there are firms out there making large profits by offering complaint investigation and resolution services. There are even people out there trying to get big settlements from corporations by 'perceiving' they are disabled and then trapping the company into a noncompliance situation. While you should never become so complacent that you don't see these types coming, we should nevertheless focus our energies on seeking out and hiring the disabled. Let me repeat. We should seek out and hire the disabled.

Do you derive a lot of satisfaction from your career? I know you hate to admit it, but much of your self-worth is tied to your job title and the paycheck you take home. It shouldn't be, but it is. Are the disabled any different? It must be sad to go through life with a serious physical or mental impairment that limits your activities, and then have this sadness reinforced by not obtaining gainful employment. There are many ways of seeking out the disabled: job fairs, disabled organizations, veterans administrations, state agencies, even word of mouth. Often, disabled people have given up on finding jobs. Actual discrimination has not occurred; but they just can't see how they would fit in with the team, and neither can the prospective employer. This is where the top-notch creative manager comes into play. (See the chapter on creativity.)

In 1997, a young man seeking a job presented himself to me. He had a special challenge because he was missing the entire lower half of his body. Due to a birth defect, the doctors had amputated his body right below the chest. He walked on his hands and sometimes used a wheelchair. I explained to him that I was willing to make reasonable accommodations, but I couldn't think of what could be done right off the bat and told him to see me the following week. In the meantime I consulted my boss. He advised me that the young man was looking for a lawsuit, and I should "make it go away." (I am still not sure how I was supposed to accomplish this.) Instead, during the next week, I worked out a plan whereby the company would build a special wheelchair with all of the whistles and bells that would allow the young man to work at the correct line height in a safe condition. The special chair took a week to build and cost five hundred dollars. The young man received his training, started to work, and became a productive employee. It was not long before he was able to get off the government dole. A few weeks down the road, my boss stated at a group meeting that he had been against hiring this disabled person, but that I had "showed them the way." To this day, it is the best compliment I have ever received. The young man won. I won. The company won and society won. How do you beat that?

Lesson from the Ranch

Everyone can spot a disability. Only a real manager can spot the wealth of talent hiding under the disability.

13

Ethics

*"Don't be fooled by those who say such things,
for 'bad company corrupts good character.'"*
1 Corinthians 15:33

*"Always do the right thing. This pacifies your family
and keeps your enemies at bay."*
Cowboy Wisdom

The result of operating a ranch without a strong value system is quickly apparent: you go out of business lickity-split. Your word is no longer your bond, and no one will purchase your livestock or extend needed credit. People will no longer hire on for work. Your neighbors distrust you. Your hopes and dreams dry up and blow away because you could not tell the difference between right and wrong. Well, maybe you could, but the lure of shortchanging someone (greed) was stronger.

I have a friend and coworker who is in his mid-fifties. I've worked with him for several years and can always depend on him to do the right thing. His ethics are never in question. We were discussing ethics at work one day when he told me a story that happened almost thirty years ago. As a young college student, he worked weekends and school breaks for an employer who encouraged his education and progression. After graduating from college, he went to work for that same employer as a full-time department manager. After about a year, a conflict developed, and he accepted a job elsewhere. Before leaving, he took a few hand tools that did not belong to him. Today, the company is no longer in existence. It closed its doors years ago. However, if the company were still in business, my friend said he would return the tools. Every time he encounters the tools in his workshop, he feels bad. The sight of them makes him feel uneasy and reminds him that, at one time, he was a thief. For me, this person has proved that he has high ethical values. This friend and coworker obeys the moral law.

Corporations often have negative outcomes because the people on board cannot tell the difference between right and wrong. Due to scope, these consequences usually take longer to materialize, but is the result the same? You can find a ton of articles and books about business ethics about businesses "losing their way," e.g., WorldCom, Tyco, Enron. You can also sign up for seminars where they preach, "do the right thing." They paint the world in stark black and white. These resources ask one-dimensional ethical questions, such as, "Should you take kickbacks from suppliers?" For me, ethics in the workplace is varying shades of gray. You have to rely on moral law: does something 'feel' wrong? It's easy to say, "There is right, and there is wrong." All major corporations have their written code of conduct. Each one is pretty much just a copy of the others and is a major dust bunny. The next time you walk into someone's office, ask to see the company code of conduct. Good luck on finding someone who will produce it within five minutes. The moral law is much easier to find and digest. It resides in each of us.

I have a problem with people stating that XYZ is an 'ethical' company or that ABC Cororation is "not an ethical company." Charles A. Reich, of the Yale Law School, states, "The corporation is an immensely powerful machine, ordered, legalistic, rational, yet utterly out of human control, wholly and perfectly indifferent to any human value." If this description is correct—and I believe it is—how can a lifeless entity be ethical? Only the people who are temporarily working there can possess a value system of right and wrong. I say temporarily because different minds and souls are constantly fluxing in and out of a corporation. If it is one of any size at all, the face of today's corporation will be different from tomorrow's, and the ethical behavior will change accordingly. I think many people confuse the ethics of a corporation with its 'culture,' the attitudes and behavior characteristic of a corporation. In large part, however, corporate cultures are a myth. So-called corporate cultures vary greatly from operation to operation or office to office. Therefore, whether you are dealing with ethics or culture, it is important to remember that it is all people-driven. Moreover, people are so diverse in their personal attitudes and behaviors that pinning a specific culture on an entire corporation is pointless. It is like trying to nail Jell-O to a wall.

Thus all ethics and morality is ultimately personal. Many people who commit ethical breaches at work actually have convinced themselves that their behavior was ethical or, at the most, a minor infraction. The real world is complex, and it is easy to lose your footing and go over the bluff. As you study the personal principles that define your values and determine your moral duty, here are some pitfalls and guide-posts:

1. **Compromise**. Right and wrong are not always clear. Beware of people who would have you compromise so you are bringing together a little of your right and a little of their wrong. This happens far too often, and it is a slippery slope.

2. **Personal Benefits**. If your activity or a decision you make results in a benefit for you personally and not just the corporation, you are probably engaging in unethical behavior. I realize that you really want that new trolling motor, but let it go.

3. **Appearance Matters.** The perception of unethical behavior on your part can destroy you just the same as actual unethical behavior. If others think you have crossed over, set them straight. Never joke about such matters. Your reputation and ability to pay the bills are at stake. Do you want to trade those for a quick laugh?

4. **See No Evil, Hear No Evil, and Speak No Evil.** Do you think isolating yourself and allowing others around you to engage in bad behavior will somehow make you an ethical island in the midst of managerial mischief? Think again. When the corporate ship sinks, everyone goes down. Speak up, and let someone know that there is a fox in the henhouse. Don't worry about the 'feelings' of the people you report. They have no respect for you or themselves.

5. **The Truth, the Whole Truth, and Nothing but the Truth**. Try viewing the truth on a sliding scale from one to ten. One equals a blatant lie, and ten is the whole truth. Most of us operate around six or seven. Ethics in the workplace would be far less of a problem if we all operated at ten. (An amazing aspect of Truth is its extreme rarity. For every true statement, there are a limitless number of false statements. The false statement may be

the result of an honest mistake or a willful deception. Regardless, submerging the true statement is an avalanche of false statements. Like searching for diamonds, finding the truth sometimes takes an enormous effort on your part. Those of us willing to invest the time and effort to search will succeed; those who don't, will fail.)

6. **Trust Your Instincts**. They will never lead you wrong. An entire lifetime of learning, observing, behaving, listening, acting, is trying to tell you something stinks. When your intuition speaks, listen. It is the wisest advisor you will ever have.

7. **Trust.** Someone with authority over you has asked you to engage in a questionable act. He or she gives you a nudge and a wink. You are one of the team, the tribe. You need to play ball with the rest of us. If you decide to go along, you have just sold your soul. In addition, how can you expect proper treatment when your boss commits ethical breaches? It is time to resign.

8. **Legal.** How many times have you heard, "It's not illegal, is it?" This should be a serious red flag. It is true, many unethical behaviors are legal, but they are still going against the grain of your personal values and beliefs. You may not wind up in court, but the fiddler is always paid. In *Othello*, Shakespeare wrote, "Reputation, reputation, reputation! O! I have lost my reputation. I have lost the immortal part of myself, and what remains is bestial." Shakespeare understood the price.

Recently, we were having a discussion on the values and ethics of new workers. One of my associates suggested we provide our corporate code of conduct to everyone arriving at our store. Another associate pointed out that we used to do this, but these booklets were expensive and we had stopped the practice due to the high cost. Suppressing a chuckle, I remarked that we would like to have values, but the price was too high. I thought this was funny, but no one was laughing.

Lesson from the Ranch

Listen for the still, small voice. It will always guide you to do the right thing.

Fads... No Thanks

"History merely repeats itself. It has all been done before.
Nothing under the sun is truly new."
Ecclesiastes 1:9

"Never train a bull to yodel. It wastes your time and infuriates the bull."
Cowboy Wisdom

Ranchers go through fads the same as everyone else. The difference is that they are much slower to implement a fad, so it takes a long time for a fad to take root. Once rooted, however, a fad becomes a way of life, and thus loses its fad status. Still, fads do arise in the ranch world, with people going crazy over specific breeds or cross-breeds. They will rip out the grasses that have sustained the ranch for years and go with the latest and greatest new thing. However, real change is slow, and when the change finally does take place, you can rest assured that it gives the best results for the money. That is the mindset, and it is not going to change today or in a hundred years.

American business, on the other hand, is addicted to fads. Everyone is under tremendous pressure to run faster and be smarter, leaner, and meaner, so any newfangled business or industry fad coming down the pike looks like salvation. These fads seldom have any lasting impact on business. Popping into existence everywhere, they just as quickly vanish. They pop in and out like virtual particles in the vacuum of space. When fads roll out, there is a fever for them exhibited by a flushed face and exaggerated zeal. Overnight, seminars and workshops pop up (usually in Las Vegas). Top management is concerned that if they don't jump aboard, the competition will be using the newest fad against them, leaving them eating dust. Teams form. Internal implementation plans are developed. 'Train the trainer' sessions are rampant. Training for employees is conducted at a frenzied pace. Entire departments spring up to drive the new fad and track its progress. Management gets plum giddy as they advocate the glory of the fad's effectiveness. Then, the new fad dies on the vine, and it is business as usual.

The assembly line process started by Henry Ford may be the last fad adopted industry-wide that is still in use. I would like to report that Edward Deming's work had a lasting impression, and it has, but only in small pockets. All fads die and fade away. No one can dispute that fads usually have a positive impact at first, but part of this is due to the Hawthorne effect. (See the chapter on consultants.)

One thing of interest is peeling back the layers of all fads. I find that they are, at the heart, the same package but with different wrapping paper. All boil down to Management 101, which is to plan, control, and lead.

The fads of the past thirty years have valid points and could serve as genuinely excellent business tools. Their failure is rooted in us, not in them. The fads ensure we have the right amount of discipline in our system, but, more importantly, they do need the element of time. In our short-term mindset, time is the one element we refuse to allot. Therefore, until we change our mindset and start focusing on strategic growth and improvement, I have decided not to play anymore. By this, I mean I refuse to get excited. Top management, by their nature, like to react and change based on short-term results, and are unable to truly commit to a new process or system even though the current system is on life support. However, if the team decides that fad A is a wonderful thing, I will saddle up and ride with the herd. Just don't expect me to be passionate about it. I have wasted far too much of my time and energy on the 'fad of the month,' and sometime back I had what alcoholics refer to as a moment of clarity (apologies to Jules Winnfield). If we would only realize that we are not working with children or criminals; or, even better, if we could realize that the people we manage are mature, intelligent adults who seek reward and praise, the same as you and I.

I ransacked my files and developed the following list of formalized 'fads' that I have been involved in since the 1970s. I hope my comments don't bring on lawsuits. (See the chapter on legal issues.)

- **Zinger Miller** – 1985 – I got a neat cardholder in which to keep my reminder cards. I now use the holder for business cards.

- **SMIP** – Statistical Methods to Improve Process – 1991 – Everyone got a certificate and a racing jacket. The program never made it to implementation.

- **TQT** – Total Quality Transformation – 1987 – I remember the binder was gray, big, and never used.

- **One-minute Management** – 1983 – They made us read the book, and then we had to walk around handing out artificial praise that was half-hearted and not very well **received**. We were forced into doing something that **was** supposed to come naturally. An enema **comes** to mind. (My wife asked me to take this **reference** out of the book, but the analogy was just too good.) It is a wonderful book, but our implementation was horrid.

- **Theory Y** – 1988 – They sold this as a soft approach that relied on everyone doing what came naturally to him or her. For me, this meant sleeping late and watching too much TV. We implemented this approach for a while until a critical customer fell out, and then we had to "get back to business."

- **Quality Circles** – 1976 – This was the first 'workshop' I attended. It was based on a Japanese method of manufacturing; it was poorly understood. The team I was on could never get past the point that it did not involve actually sitting around in a circle. We never grasped the concept and let it die gracefully after a couple of months. I recall that we did have many conversations at our meetings about us dropping the 'big one' on Japan back in 1945 and how we might need to do it again just to show them that they're not better than us with all this Quality Circle fluff. Americans—gotta love 'em.

- **Continuous Improvement** – 2003 – Based on the fourteen-point Deming philosophy, its use waxes and wanes with every crisis. The better companies strive to maintain its status outside these critical periods. Most don't. I've seen the CI process go by the wayside too many times. However, I am still pulling for the better companies.

- **Total Quality Management** – 1992 – Continuous improvement on steroids. A well-meaning management guide to problem solution but too many tools and too much math for the regular Joe. Also involves great amounts of discipline. Years ago, I used to teach this course to various companies via the community college. I have no idea if the companies continued to use this process through the years. However, I would not bet the ranch that they did.

- **MBO** – Management by Objectives – 1985 – I thought this was why we were getting a check in the first place. Anyway, the formal system involved too much face time and was hard to determine the level of reward based on the result. When you get through establishing the incident objectives and selecting the appropriate strategy and the tactical direction for the strategy, you are ready to check out to the funny farm. "Let's see, three down, and only two hundred more employees to go." No wonder it never took off. If given the time, this system is one of the best tools available. However, who does have time for this? We are too busy explaining our quarterly losses.

- **Matrix Management** – 1999 – Well-meaning people claim it works. However, like a UFO, I hear what they are saying, but I have never seen one. The problem is obviously too much dual reporting going on with too many dotted lines. This is wisdom that has been around in print for around two thousand years (Matthew 6:24). Unless you have a polished, mature team, you are asking for trouble.

- **Team-based Management** – I don't have any personal experience with this however, I have a couple of friends in two industries who swear by the team-based management approach. There were no supervisors in sight; just a lot of hand-holding while singing *This Land is Your Land*. Both factories are now closed, and the unsupervised, team-based employees are history.

- **Process Re-engineering** – I've been involved with this concept several times. It sounds mysterious, but it really just means how to move your widget from A to B in the shortest, quickest distance. My experience with process re-engineering is that it 1) tends to backslide and 2) you find your layout and processes are not the problem, your people are. You must be prepared to re-engineer your process every few years as your customers, specifications, or products change. Proper process re-engineering is day-to-day rather than a singular project. Listen to your supervisors and workers. Then do what they suggest.

So what should we do? The first thing is to give up trying to implement every new fad as it arrives. Good business is not about fads, catchy slogans, or glittery objects. It is about only two things: one is your people, and the other is your customers. If you simply apply the Golden Rule to both groups, you will never need anything else. Let the fads be someone else's problem as you report record profits, add more jobs, and grow the business.

Lesson from the Ranch

Fads are like cattle stampedes. Everyone participates, there is a lot of dust and noise; and at the end, you find yourself miles from your goal. Don't follow the herd. Search instead for excellence.

Firing

"Even while we were with you, we gave you this command: "
Those unwilling to work will not get to eat."
2 Thessalonians 3:10-12

"It doesn't take a genius to spot a goat in a flock of sheep."
Cowboy Wisdom

Years ago, one of the big wheels where I worked seemed to have it all. He had ridden on the coat tails of the man above him and had situated himself in a secure position with a good salary, stock options, and an annual six-figure bonus. He served on numerous boards and was active in industry associations. He had a great wife, great kids, and a mid-size, paid-off ranch. He loved the ranch more than anything. It was always his favorite topic. Once his old mentor left the company, however, the big wheel found himself suddenly exposed. The people in the ivory tower now viewed him as low-hanging fruit. He was weighed, measured, and found wanting. Termination was on the menu for him that day.

Lacking the spit and polish usually associated with people in his position, he found that he could get interviews based on his résumé strength but could not nail the face-to-face interviews. He became more and more frustrated and started to drift into depression. He started taking missteps in life that resulted in a divorce, the loss of his children, and finally the loss of his beloved ranch. I don't know where he is now. People who knew him have lost track. He seems to have fallen off the face of the Earth. All this happened in a thirty-six month period. Imagine what can happen to someone who does not possess the college degree or the polished résumé, and who has a huge mortgage along with hungry mouths at home.

We must never forget that terminating someone is a major life event and can lead to his or her destruction. It ranks right up there with death and divorce. I would wager that each reader of this book can recall a similar event whereby someone's life went down the drain after a termination. As people professionals, I believe we must be personally involved in every decision to terminate. That also means we are willing and able to stand our ground against a crowd crying for blood. This is a very difficult position to be in, but remember, leaders often stand alone. I have found that when you stand up against the authorities you gain even more respect. Maybe not that same day, but it will come.

For some morbid reason, a good number of the people in power secretly derive pleasure from firing someone or causing someone's demise. I suppose it makes them feel—for a fleeting minute—more powerful and in charge. This adrenaline boost makes up for their inability to manage and lead. I know this is true and beyond debate. I have seen far too many gleeful smiles and excited eyes. It is sad when you realize that peers and associates sometimes gain pleasure from someone getting the ax. This is especially true in the below-average companies. There, the employees are the walking dead. After someone leaves, the remaining employees reflect on their boring lives. They consider how trapped they are in dead-end jobs. Nevertheless, they think, at least they are not stupid enough to be fired like their unfortunate friend. Moreover, this narrow escape seems to boost their self-esteem for a day or two.

Don't get me wrong. I believe that some people need firing. Indeed, some are begging for it, and I like to give people what they want. The reasons someone would seek termination are varied and often make no sense except to them. To examine these people and their reasoning would require another book. To put it in ranch lingo, "only cows know why they stampede." Suffice it to say, while this is a strange lot, their numbers are small; though not so rare that you won't encounter them. You need to recognize them for what they are and move on. In addition, if someone is just begging for termination in order to sue, go ahead and make his or her day. Be sure to remind the person to add wrongful termination to the suit. (See bobbing a dog's tail in the chapter on decisions.)

Too often, managers sweat blood satisfying the just cause tests. Did we provide notice that the behavior was against the rules? Was it a reasonable rule? Did we do a timely and fair investigation? Does the evidence support the charge? Did we treat everyone equally, or did we target specific individuals or groups? Does the penalty meet the crime? Is it an eye for eye? Once you have met the criteria for just cause, you should fire the person and move on.

But should we? Is it possible that a person and his or her life are a little more than the sum of just cause? It is easy to check off the just cause items, but does it really mean anything? Do we really know the person and the circumstances?

If only we realized that when we terminate, we have failed. Let me rephrase: when you lose an employee, you didn't do your job correctly. You botched another good opportunity. Instead of enriching someone's life, you didn't take the time to care about the person. That sounds like simplistic thinking. Who can dispute it? One could say that the person was given ample warnings with the progressive disciplinary process, and thus fired himself. Incompetent managers often use that lame excuse. It makes us feel better when we can say it was the employee's entire fault. Like Pilate, we can wash our hands and move on to devastate more people tomorrow. The truth is, once discipline starts, you have already lost the employee, and ninety percent of the time, you will not get him back. Progressive discipline only drags out the result. I know that the mantra is supposed to be that discipline is not to punish but to correct, and I know that some managers are able to use it sparingly and wisely, with good results. I also know that most fail at discipline.

In your career, you will see the Peter Principle come into play. The Peter Principle is a theory by Dr. Laurence J. Peter whereby employees advance to their highest level of competence, then are promoted to a level where they are incompetent. They then stay in that position, wreaking havoc on all around them. Once companies realize what is going on, most employers will start making moves to terminate this person to correct past mistakes. Remember, though: it was the employer who made the mistake. In my mind, very little fault can be placed at such an employee's feet. Who wouldn't want a promotion with better pay? Who among us is willing to step forward and proclaim ourselves incompetent? No, it is the employer's mistake to correct; therefore, we correct by reassignment with the applicable pay adjustment, not by termination. In fact, your organization's guidelines on internal promotions should come with one *get out of jail* card. This guideline will take a lot of pressure off the internal candidate and give the employer an easier route for correcting their mistake if needed.

90

Once all else has failed and you are moving into the actual process of firing, the way the termination is carried out is very important. It is important that it is done in a way that leaves the employee their dignity, while at the same time limiting the company's exposure to lawsuits or arbitration. I try to live by a rule that many often don't follow. That rule is simple: **Hire slow / fire fast.** Once we know the person must go, act as quickly as possible. Dragging out the process is unprofitable for the organization, damages the other employees, and is extremely unkind to the person targeted for termination. Cut the cord and let the person get on with his or her life. More times than not, the employee is miserable at work. Employees can sense the impending doom (see the chapter "Spritually Connected"), so severing the tie takes a tremendous burden off them.

For the actual termination, I offer the following guidelines:

1. Limit the knowledge of the termination to the person, their boss, and human resources.

2. Depending on the demeanor of the boss, you decide who speaks. I would recommend that human resources carry the water.

3. Call the person into the office. Take the phone off the hook, turn off your cellphone, and close the door. Don't be concerned about the day of the week or the hour of the day. Some fools believe the day and time is important, i.e., "It's best to fire someone Friday afternoon at four." This is baloney and not even sliced. You can, however, tell them that sociologists have determined that cutting off your big toe is best performed on Wednesdays at 9:30 AM. That should keep them busy for a few days and out of your hair.

4. Inform the person that you are letting him or her go for [insert reason]. Don't make it personal. Avoid remarks that make the person feel he or she has failed (remember, the employee didn't—you did). Limit your comments to statements about the job not being a good fit due to [see above reason].

5. Once the reason is given, you should not discuss the matter. The person will want to talk but now is not the time. Remember to advise the boss that any discussion should not take place. This is the point where smooth terminations fail, tempers flare, and we lose control of the situation. Allowing the person to discuss the matter usually escalates, and in the end he or she will go straight from your office to the nearest lawyer.

6. Stand up, signaling the event is over.

7. If a severance package is involved, direct the person to the office where someone else will discuss the pre-arranged details. The people involved in the actual termination should never perform severance detail discussion.

I have certainly botched my share of terminations in the past. Usually it was because I was doing the firing in anger. I have learned to sleep on it for a day or two. Once or twice, I've fired someone in a very unprofessional manner, disregarding my own advice. This involved a couple of people whom I intensely disliked, and I allowed it to show. I should be ashamed. Nowadays, when I find myself in this situation, I hand the baton to someone else. I cannot hide my feelings very well, so why pour gas on the fire?

On the ranch, we have a guidepost that goes something like this, "When you give a lesson in meanness to a critter or a person, don't be surprised if they learn their lesson."

Lesson from the Ranch

When we have to fire, it usually means we have failed.

16

Fun at Work

"A time to cry and a time to laugh. A time to grieve and a time to dance."
Ecclesiastes 3:4

"To ride or not to ride? What a stupid question!"
Cowboy Wisdom

I am blessed with a son and son-in-law who love ranch work like a pig loves mud. We boil in the summer and freeze in the winter. Problems and challenges pop up that we must resolve. Equipment breaks down, which causes a spike in the blood pressure. Throughout it all, we have fun. We joke, we laugh, and nothing is too serious. We try to place everything in its proper perceptive. At the end of the day, we feel good and look forward to tomorrow's adventure. They and I look forward to the work in large part because it is fun and we enjoy working together. The work exercises our bodies, and the fun refreshes our minds. This combination of work and play is what makes a successful ranch. There is a ranch close to mine called "Happy Ranch." There is another one nearby called "Silly Ass Ranch." They raise donkeys. (Get it?)

Dad subscribed to *Progressive Farmer* magazine and read each article. One of these articles suggested that a person could tie a bunch of old tires together and pull these behind the tractor, thereby spreading the cowpiles (bovine fecal material). Not only would the fertilizer help the land, but since a cow would not eat around his or her own cow manure piles, dispersing these actually would—in a small way—increase the grazable acreage. Therefore Dad tied several old tires together, and away he went. He soon found that the tires did not have enough weight to disrupt the cowpiles. (Do you see where this is going?) So Dad instructed me to 'ride the tires' while he drove around the pastures. Talk about a crappy job. In addition to all the bumping and struggling to maintain a handhold, I was constantly splattered with the fresh piles. Once we were finished, I looked like a stack of cow manure stacked several feet high. It also took a week for my tail to heal. Here's the kicker. I loved it. It was more fun than anything I had done in a long time. (This was before my hormones kicked in.) From that point on I pestered Dad on a regular basis, reminding him that the cowpiles needed spreading again. My point is this: everything is relative. A job that may appear to be straight from the bowels of hell may in fact be a very enjoyable experience for someone with the proper mindset.

I can tell you straight away that if I work for an organization that doesn't value having a little fun and fails to see that fun contributes to the bottom line, I will be leaving for somewhere that does. Life is far too short to spend your time—your most valuable resource—whiling away the hours at a depressing, humorless worksite. When I speak of fun, I am not talking about foolishness. I don't mean walking around in clown suits or shooting each other with water pistols. I also don't think fun entails mocking or belittling someone. I am talking about two types of fun only. The first is engaging in interesting, absorbing, challenging work. The second is simple, pointless fun.

We cannot invent or force fun. It comes naturally out of a good working environment. The top managers at the location create this environment. I have had the great pleasure of working with many top managers who had a lot of fun while they worked. When I reflect on the health of the organizations where fun was a natural part of the business, in every case the bottom line was solid, business was growing, and retention was high.

Conversely, I once worked for one large corporation where every day was doom and gloom. Not only was no one having fun, but the days consisted of back-stabbing and jockeying for political position. The turnover was high, morale was bad, and stress hung over us like a black cloud. I noted this during my interview. Nevertheless, my motivation was the salary increase (greed). After twelve weeks, I offered my resignation as department manager and accepted a position at another firm that valued fun. My new salary was twenty percent less than my previous salary. My new employer did not realize it, but I would have moved for even less. As previously stated, life is far too short. Since then, I have made up the difference in money tenfold. I can just imagine how my life would have been had I not resigned. I would have endured untold misery for a handful of dollars.

Lesson from the Ranch

If fun is not part of the equation, you can ride the trail by yourself.

Government

"They plan to topple me from my high position. They delight in telling lies about me. They praise me to my face but curse me in their hearts."
Psalms 62:4

"Tellin' the deputy to git lost and makin' 'em do it are two entirely different propositions."
Cowboy Wisdom

A s discussed in the chapter on consultants, the government and its many resources can be a big help to ranchers. I have always found government employees to be overworked, underpaid, and yet full of pride, cheerfully providing assistance when and if they can. Nevertheless, most ranchers avoid the government as if it were the Black Death. That's the nature of cowboys. They are staunchly independent and don't want anyone getting in their business. Some of this attitude the government deserves. It is notorious for stepping over the line with overzealous authority. Sometimes the conflicts are environmental. I cannot imagine anyone who is a better steward of the environment than the ranchers and hunters. However, to listen to some bureaucrats tell it, you would think ranchers had horns and a tail. Actually, only a few of them do, and they mostly live in Oklahoma.

The relationship between business and government is no different. We tend to exaggerate the difficulties the government puts on us with all the rules and regulations. I'll admit that I dislike any government regulation. I believe that any time a law or regulation hits the books, we lose some of our freedom. Nevertheless, I also will admit that without these parameters, too many managers and owners would swing the pendulum too far, and abuses would mount. There are some bad people out there. Still, I strongly disagree with many government rules and believe that many of the regulations are just plain stupid. Like a corporation, the government is really the totality of the people working there at any specific time, and people sometimes do stupid things. Let me be clear on this point. I don't think government employees are stupid. Through the years, I have gotten to know some of them on a personal level, and find them to be decent, intelligent, respectful people who are just trying to do a thankless job. There are a few government employees—albeit a minority—who are full of vainglory and like to play the "gotcha" game, but they stand out like a sore thumb. Still, the government as a whole, especially since the 1960s, has meticulously tried to void all human judgment in government matters. Instead of wise decision-makers who listen to all facets of a case, they want us to refer to a codebook for the one-size-fits-all decision. I don't know whether to be mad or sad.

Encapsulated in our various corporate policies are the details of how we deal with the government. When the EEOC, OFCCP, OSHA, EPA, NLRB, Wage and Hour, or any other of the alphabet soup of government agencies contacts us, we immediately go into our circle-the-wagons mode. We contact our lawyers and our risk management department. Everyone up and down the organizational chart wants to be 'kept in the loop.' It is a full-time job just making the daily contacts. We have to keep informing the top brass that nothing has actually happened at this point. The involved employees supply the meat of the issue to the lawyers, who then regurgitate it into some legalese form. We spoon-feed this tasteless mush back to the government. In the meantime, the gut-wrenched local managers sit around and wait for a decision, which may or may not involve their future employment. Finally, after a Wimbledon-type flurry, we reach an agreement in which a settlement for [insert four- to five-figure number] amount of dollars is offered. Everyone is informed. The lawyers ask the government to buy into the settlement. The legal folks assure everyone that the dollars spent are only of *nuisance value*. We use the term *nuisance value* so we never look guilty. We just want the fly to stay off our food. We would never actually admit that we probably kicked a cow pile on a hot day. Everyone agrees, and the lawyers mail us their bill as we crank the alert level back to orange and wait for the next incoming.

If the government and the company cannot seem to reach a settlement, the government will issue a *Right to Sue* letter to the company. This means that the government employee did not want to expend the time and energy to resolve the matter. I suspect that, sometimes, the lawyers will convolute a case to the point that nobody really knows what is going on, and who is willing to read and study a ream of legal speak? Therefore, the government employee takes the easy route and issues the *Right to Sue* notice. For the overworked government employee, life is simpler when he or she plows around the stump. In today's environment, a *Right to Sue* notice usually brings an immediate lawsuit. I swear the notice and the lawsuit cross in the mail. Once the lawsuit is filed, you lose the choice of whether to use a law firm or not. Welcome to three to four years of producing documents, giving and attending depositions, and generally running on a mouse wheel. The actors and scenery change, but the script remains the same.

Is this really the best way? Is this best for the organization and your career growth? It is unequivocally the best way for the attorneys and the government employees. The law firm gets to bill, and the bureaucrat knows how it will turn out with little work on their side. In the meantime, you and your managers sit on the sidelines, relegated to spectator status. You drink beer and eat hot dogs while you watch the Christians and lions battle it out in the arena. Win or lose, you leave the stadium in a cloud of dust and keep returning to the combat zone, where you ensure a steady supply of Christians and lions. The company picks up the entertainment tab. Good lions are expensive. Christians, not so much.

Before drinking the Kool-Aid and assuming a submissive position, I used to handle all of the government claims such as EEOC, Wage and Hour, OFCCP, and arbitrations, with little to no assistance from a law firm. I dealt directly with the agency. Once I was ready to present my case, I reviewed it with legal (always) and the labor people (only if they had a dog in the hunt). I allowed them to massage my answer to ensure clarity or to cover a legal loophole. Nevertheless, the decision to revise or modify always remained with me. Throughout the years and after handling dozens of cases, I can truthfully attest that I did not lose even one. I never paid a settlement or lost an arbitration. I never paid back pay or was forced to bring the employee back to work.

The culture changed as the years went by, and more and more corporate legal departments felt that mid-level managers were not capable of handling these issues. One day in the past, I am not sure exactly when, we looked up and found ourselves outside the loop. Well, not entirely. We were still deemed the responsible party who allowed the practice or behavior in the first place, and thus, in each claim, we suffered some smearing of our reputation. So now, I always wind up paying a 'nuisance value' or am forced to bring the employee back to work because I was incompetent in the first place and should never have discharged him or her. Okay, I am exaggerating. They only think I am incompetent half of the time.

If you handle your own cases with assistance only from the lawyers and the labor relations department, you will find that your work life is more satisfying, and you will be a better steward of the company's money. Here is why:

1. Any settlement to an employee greatly encourages others in the workforce to file claims against you.

2. Only you will have the details and—more importantly—the passion to argue your case. Unlike the lawyers, you will allow your emotions to show. In addition, the truth you deliver will be a great advantage over the legalese the government has grown accustomed to hearing.

3. I was involved in a case involving a Hispanic woman who had filed a race discrimination charge. We settled with her for $75 (this is not a typo). Obviously, she did not have a claim. How much of the bottom-line money could I have saved the company by handling this without Crane, Poole & Schmidt? How many more widgets did our employees have to produce by the sweat of their brows to pay for these lawyers?

4. Managers can develop a very lazy mindset when they know that every time they stump their toes, the cavalry will ride up with guns and billing hours blazing. How lazy would we become if we knew that the cavalry was not showing up, that we would actually have to sit in the chair and explain our own bone-headed moves? Pain is a strong motivator. You need full ownership both of responsibility and accountability so that no matter the outcome, the pain or the pleasure belongs to you.

5. When people represent themselves, you become a better manager and a better team. This in turn will cause claims to decrease drastically, thus making this entire chapter a moot issue.

Dealing directly with an issue will always produce the best outcome. At the very least, everyone will know what you did and where you stand. Moreover, it puts the government employees with whom you deal on notice that you take no prisoners. Back in the 1960s, my great-uncle, Sam Tucker, was pulling a hog trailer late at night through a small Arkansas town. Sam ran a cattle and hog ranch and was returning late from a hog sale where he had sold several head. The Arkansas State Police stopped him. The young state trooper claimed Sam had been swerving. In the trooper's advanced math, this two plus two had to equal drinking alcohol. Uncle Sam explained that he might have crossed the median line, but he had never had a drink in his entire life. The officer insisted he could smell alcohol. After a roadside argument, he arrested Uncle Sam. The hearing was presided over by a judge who had been friends with Uncle Sam for many years. He knew that Uncle Sam was a teetotaler and a highly respected rancher. The judge asked Uncle Sam if he wanted representation by legal counsel. Uncle Sam said he would handle it himself. After hearing both sides, the judge summarily dismissed the charge and told Uncle Sam that he was sorry for the mistake. Pointing to the state trooper, Uncle Sam said, "Don't feel sorry for me. Feel sorry for that SOB. He is the one that does not know the difference 'tween hog s*** and whiskey."

I often want to tell the government agencies this story, but I am sure they wouldn't get it. I suppose I should feel sorry for them, too.

Lesson from the Ranch

Like wasps, I don't spend a lot of thought on the government, I just know things are less tense when they're not around.

CHAPTER
18

Hiring

"Therefore, please command that cedars from Lebanon be cut for me. Let my men work alongside yours, and I will pay your men whatever wages you ask. As you know, there is no one among us who can cut timber like you Sidonians!"
1 King 5:6

"Never hire a man who wears gloves and smokes cigarettes. He'll spend way too much time pulling off his gloves and rolling cigarettes."
Cowboy Wisdom

During the big cattle drives in the late 1800s, the cattle barons hired hundreds of seasoned cowboys. The typical Hollywood movie doesn't reveal this fact, but many cowboys were black and Mexican. The trail bosses could not care less about race, age, or religion. They only wanted cowboys who could move the cattle in the safest and fastest time. Most of the cowboys were known by the various ranches and carried their reputations with them. In fact, a new cowboy would have a hard time lining up a job unless another cowboy was willing to vouch for him. Vouching for someone was serious business, as you staked your integrity and future employment on the new cowboy's performance. This was peer pressure at its height. If the new cowboy couldn't cut the mustard, he was cut loose, sometimes with the pay he was owed. Cattle drives are no place to mollycoddle a poor performer.

Like the trail bosses, I have one steadfast rule in this arena: **Hire slow / fire fast.** As long as I stand by my own rule, things go as planned. When I violate my rule, I always pay the price. I hire slow for two main reasons.

The first is that I want to ensure that the new person is truly needed. Many times, I have found that through job combination or restructuring we can eliminate the position altogether. This should always be our goal when someone leaves a position. It should be our goal even before someone leaves, but his or her departure opens a unique window for us to observe. Anytime you eliminate a position, you have obviously eliminated another person. Each person you hire will hopefully bring good things with him or her, but there will also be negative baggage, simply because all of us have baggage, whether we admit to it or not. Sometimes it's just a simple matter of the organization not really needing that particular position. Maybe it was necessary back in 1985 but not today. Maybe it was a friend of a friend placed into that slot. Hire slow, observe closely, and you'll be able to determine if the position really needs to be filled.

The other reason I hire slow is that I want to ensure that we have a good fit. The person, the culture, and the job should line up in a near-perfect alignment. You are never going to get the ideal person for any position, but you can take your time and get close. The closer the alignment, the more likely the new person will be successful.

During this initial phase, many interviewers get frustrated because of the limitations placed on them by the federal and state governments. Unless you construct your questions in bizarre ways or any of the following directly relate to the position, you'll be skirting discrimination violations when you ask questions about age, citizenship, disabilities, credit, arrest record, English skills, education, driver's license, height, weight, club memberships, religion, union affiliation, veteran status, … and the list of subjects to avoid continues ad nauseam.

So if you cannot ask an applicant relevant questions, how do you determine who to select and hire? I think the key lies in the word 'relevant'. While we tend to get in an uproar over the questions we cannot ask, how relevant can they be in the first place? What difference does it make to me what religion is observed by the applicants? Unless I am hiring them as a translator or English teacher, why should I care about their language skills? Outside of criminal convictions, which we can ask about (felonies), what do their youthful mistakes and arrest records have to do with anything? Maybe the police were harassing them. Maybe racial profiling was involved. All I want is to move my hay from the field to the barn. Why do I care about a driver's license? How they get to work is their problem. Obviously, they have a plan, or they wouldn't be applying for the position. In addition, if they don't have a plan, that is still not my concern. Unless your company policy states that you will personally go around and pick up everyone who doesn't have a driver's license, then you don't have a dog in the hunt.

For me, what matters is that I get a glimpse into the real person behind the interview façade. In spite of the experts' advice that only job-related questions should be asked, I discuss a variety of topics with open-ended questions that allow me such a glimpse. Then I base my decision or recommendation based on the following attributes, listed in order of importance.

1. **Attitude.** I know you are probably sick and tired of hearing about the importance of attitude. Well, you had better get ready to hear it again. I ask questions about beliefs and values. I seek to discover dispositions to act in certain ways,. because I want a partner who has an optimistic, encouraging, upbeat attitude. I need a team member who sees the world as one full of opportunities and has a driving curiosity as to how he or she can make it better.

2. **Integrity**. I need and desire honesty and consistent decency. I want a professional who has morals; someone whom I will never have to worry about as to which path he or she will take when tempted.

3. **Confidence.** *Not* cockiness or self-flattery. (It is a fine line the applicant walks in an interview.) The organization cannot prosper if we don't have individuals who fully believe in themselves and their abilities. I search for people who feel comfortable in their own skin and who will be willing to challenge the status quo.

4. **Appearance.** This may sound elitist, but if you come to an interview with face piercings, tattoos and a green Mohawk while wearing a tank top and shorts, there is a distinct likelihood that I am not hiring you for our EEOC compliance officer position. While appearance in itself is somewhat relevant to the job, people who groom themselves, make sure their clothes are washed, mended, and ironed, and sit up straight in the chair stand a much better chance of a job offer and—history has proven—will make superior

long-term employees. They have shown respect for the company and the position. I don't care how poor you are; you can always clean up. If my behavior is discriminatory, then so be it.

5. **Résumé.** Résumés are of limited value. Everyone inflates the good stuff and leaves out the bad. It is only helpful when making the initial determinations screenings by quickly assessing the applicant's education and experience. Other than that, enter the résumé in the system, file it away, and don't use it during the interview. It has always surprised me to see interviewers going over people's résumés, asking them questions based on the résumés. You already have that information. Why rehash it? Spend your valued time exploring the actual person sitting in front of you.

I used to conduct interviews in the traditional way. I would always be under pressure to fill the job within the two weeks rule. This was a rule that I gave *power* to because I accepted it without question. I reviewed résumés and brought in the short list of three to four applicants to interview. I sat behind my desk, keeping all the power while the applicant sat in front of the desk. We exchanged pleasantries and cracked a few lame jokes to clear the air. We laughed at my jokes and not so much at their attempt at humor. The overly nervous applicant would answer my boilerplate questions with boilerplate answers while I reviewed his boilerplate résumé. Depending on my mood and/or the nature of the position, a tour of the facilities might be involved. These tours I sometimes delegated to a subordinate. I was far too important to actually stroll among the unwashed masses. During this time, it was common practice to schedule the applicant to interview with several other managers, whose opinions I rarely learned. Afterwards, in my 'important voice,' I informed the applicant that we had several others to interview, and we would be in contact. Then I scheduled the next person to torture. In the end, I picked the applicant who seemed the most willing to follow the crowd, thus ensuring a continuation of mindless control over the workforce. It was also important that the new hire didn't seem too confident or too intelligent. These types wouldn't be happy and would move elsewhere after the first year, so why waste our time?

Now, obviously, the previous paragraph is an exaggeration. However, broken into pieces, how much of it actually happens every day?

As the years have rolled by, I have developed more of a ranch approach to hiring. I still do the review of résumés and create the short list based on education and experience. However, when it comes to the interview, I remove the formality. We conduct the interview while looking at the facility(s), at breakfast or at lunch, and while driving around. If I need more time, I take the applicant to dinner and invite along a few of my peers. At the office, I do at least eighty percent of the interview on the tailgate of my truck. I ask very few job-related questions. Based on education and experience, I know they are competent and whatever knowledge they lack, we can readily provide. I don't ask questions as much as just talk. We have general discussions about general things. Besides, if they will be reporting to someone other than me, the manager of that area will be asking the competence questions. At the end of the process, my gut instinct quickly tells me the best choice for the position. Don't belabor the issue; go with your basic intuition. The only battle ahead is with the area manager, who will often base his decision on the résumé alone. I don't always pick the candidate who looks most qualified on paper. I might have an applicant with advanced degrees and years of hands-on experience with the some of the best companies. Nevertheless, if he is a jerk, or lazy, or absent, I don't have much. Just because a chicken has wings doesn't mean it can fly.

This chapter focuses on salaried individuals. Although hiring hourly employees at a large facility may not allow you the time and effort that you place into hiring managers, your processes and thoughts should be the same. Attitude, integrity, confidence, and appearance should be more important than a stuffed résumé or a ballooned application.

When you're hiring for hourly positions, does the first-line management do the hiring? If not, why not? Human resources should play their part in collecting and vetting applicants, ensuring that all the paperwork is correct, and that the person is legal to work, enrolled in the appropriate insurance, and so on. Nevertheless, the actual interview and job offers should come from the first-line supervisors in the areas you are hiring. They will do a much better job of selecting applicants for hire. They should have ownership of the process from A to Z. First-line supervisors often claim that the company is *scraping the bottom of the barrel* and providing poor new hires. Insisting that the supervisor do the hiring removes this crutch. The only rub with this process is the initial reluctance of the supervisors, as they will claim they don't have time. As they see the turnover trend downward and the quality trend upward, they will wonder why they were not doing this all along. Not only will the supervisors do a better job of hiring (and retaining), but employees appreciate working for the people who hired them and don't feel like they have been 'stuck' with bad supervisors. How would you feel if you entered a new job and then never saw the person who interviewed and hired you?

Another lesson from the ranch is to segregate the new hires the first week before you expose them to the general workforce. This is especially true if you work in a manufacturing environment containing hundreds or even thousands of workers. Keeping the new hires together as a small group and not throwing them to the wolves the first few days can go a long way in keeping these people around for a while. The first week would be an ideal time for any necessary training classes. It doesn't matter what you manufacture, initial training is always a good investment. This could involve plant tours, meeting with other departments, or visiting with top management to find out their philosophies. On the ranch, when new cattle arrive, we keep them in the corral or in a separate pasture from the herd. This gives them time to settle down and learn the sights and smells of their new home. If you don't corral or pen them, they'll spend the first few days fighting with the herd and using every resource they have to escape the fences. Isolating the new cattle also gives the rancher time to give them extra attention. The rancher can get used to the new cattle, and more importantly, the new cattle can get used to the rancher. Corral your new employees their first few days so you can hand feed them and let them see that you mean no harm. Did he just compare people to cattle? Yes, I did. All social creatures have the same basic instincts, and we should observe and learn from all.

No matter how much time and effort we put into our hiring efforts, we will sometimes make mistakes. Sometimes the person is able to fool us by amplifying strengths and hiding weaknesses. This happens in other areas of life as well. As Samuel Rogers said, back in 1860, "It doesn't signify whom one marries, for one is sure to find next morning that it was someone else." When this happens, remember the rule: *Hire slow / Fire fast.*

Lesson from the Ranch

Slow and steady is the way to effectively drive cattle and productively hire people.

19

Labor Relations

"Can two people walk together without agreeing on the direction?"
Amos 3:3

"When you're throwin' your weight around, be ready to have it thrown
around by somebody else."
Cowboy Wisdom

A cattle ranch has no place for labor relations. It hasn't been needed, wanted, or desired. There is an unwritten rule that has been in place for centuries in the agricultural world: if you don't work, you don't eat. Conversely, there is compassion in the agricultural world that is unmatched anywhere else. Farmers and ranchers take care of people in need. If an employee or a neighbor falls on hard times, farmers and ranchers will help them to their feet. If there is a family down the road that is having trouble feeding their kids or buying clothes, the rural community will be there.

Unfortunately, the business world doesn't always follow this model. If people don't work, the unions will protect them by wallpapering management with grievance and arbitrations. You stand little chance of prevailing even with a rock-solid case, as many of the arbitrators are from the world of academia. The left-leaning liberals will employ every tactic available to ensure the gold-brickers keep their jobs. Therefore, if they don't work, they still eat. I am certainly not referring to every arbitrator as bad. I have run across a few wise, conservative-minded arbitrators. However, when I speak in harsh tones about arbitrators, I am speaking of them as a general population, not individually. As stated in the chapter on government, your best defense is to present the case yourself. Your passion for right and wrong may even break through their foggy minds. On the other hand, when employees need a helping hand to weather a rough spot in life, our corporate policies often limit our ability to help. Everyone must be treated the same, so exceptions to the policies and rules are frowned upon. To complicate matters, the various unions will also throw up roadblocks when you try to help someone in need. If it involves any compensation or a tweak of the work rules, they will scream to high heaven that everyone deserves these "special favors," thus tying your hands.

The history of labor relations in the United States goes back several years. Somewhere along the line, the company president's doctor advised him to never deal directly with unions, thereby creating a VP of Labor Relations. As stated by Robert Townsend in *Further Up the Organization*, "Under him [the VP of Labor Relations], a whole swarm of people got on the payroll with a vested interest in keeping management and labor sore at each other. In that regard, they have the same goal as the union leadership." I don't really believe this, but there may be some truth to it.

If some of your employees are unionized, you should have two objectives that you work toward every day. The first objective comes from the old saying, "Keep your friends close and your enemies even closer." Whenever possible, work with the union to achieve your organizational goals. Defining them as the enemy may sound a bit harsh, but their underlying goals and your goals are polar opposites. They want to protect seniority, load you down with tons of needless classifications, and ensure that the slackers maintain their employment. The only common thread is that both sides need the organization to profit, keeping the stockholders happy while ensuring a steady flow of union dues.

Working with unions may entail sharing more information than you are used to doing. They need to know where the business stands and what role they can play in its success. If you treat the union leadership as mature, responsible adults and sincerely ask for their help, you just might get it. Still, don't lose sight of the fact that their primary purpose in life is to collect union dues. The smart manager will weave this fact throughout every request for help. (If you don't believe the union dues theory, just threaten to stop dues Check Off on your next contract and see how fast the national leadership will strike.)

One tactic that I have favored through the years is to paper them with at least as many company proposals as they are sure to have. I learned long ago not to sit down at the bargaining table with only three or four proposals in hand while they have fifty to a hundred. I know many negotiation experts disagree with me, but I like some amount of quid pro quo, and it also keeps them from knowing my strategy. A side benefit is that it keeps them busy while making their heads spin. As Edward Noyes Westcott said, "They say a reasonable amount o' fleas is good fer a dog; keeps him from broodin' over bein' a dog." I love that reasoning. Keep them scratching while we are strategizing.

The second objective is to cultivate decertification. In my experience, at least eighty percent of employees would prefer to deal directly with management without all the restraints of a union. At some point in the past, the organization was not open and fair or at least not perceived this way by employees, and that was when the union moved in. If you have now restored a culture of openness and fairness, you have a good possibility of throwing the union back out. As with any action involving the National Labor Relations Board, use extreme caution in fostering this movement. Nevertheless, with a lot of work and a bit of luck, you can accomplish this goal. You should aim for it for your employees' and shareholders' sake. There is no higher job satisfaction for a manager than having a successful grass-roots decertification.

When you have unions, you must engage in collective bargaining. In this area, I adhere whenever possible to a few guidelines:

1. Never bring a knife to a gunfight. The unions bring in professional negotiators, who bargain day in and day out. Don't let local management, who may only negotiate every three to five years, even attempt to cross swords with these pros. Always use a company spokesperson who negotiates several contracts a year. Trying to be your own spokesperson is like performing surgery on yourself. You are not qualified. Even though it looks easy, you have too much invested to be rational and objective once it goes wrong.

2. While the spokesperson carries the water, remember that you own the well. You may find that you have as much trouble keeping the spokesperson in line as carrying through your negotiation strategy. Regardless of the situation, the spokesperson works for management.

3. The spokesperson will—or should—have sidebar discussions with the union leadership. Make sure

you capture all agreements in writing with everyone signing off. Left flat-footed after the negotiations by nebulous side agreements, I finally learned my lesson. As Samuel Goldwyn said, "An oral agreement isn't worth the paper it's written on."

4. Real power is never given; we take it. Remember that the company always has the ultimate power. The union can only bleed you if you say yes to their proposal. Sometimes you may negotiate to impasse, but I will take a deadlock any day versus saying yes to something the company doesn't agree with. As Nancy Reagan said, "Just say no." As you strip away all the layers, you will find it is just that easy.

5. To run with the big dogs, you have to leave the porch. Be willing to absorb a lockout or a strike. I have been in situations before when the CEO has given a clear directive that he is not willing to accept a strike, and that the negotiating team is not to even glance down that path. When this happens, I feel like my mother's old cat: neutered, declawed, and not allowed to play outside. Moreover, just like my mother's cat, I find myself sitting and staring into space, only breaking my trance for lunch.

6. You will draw more flies with sugar than vinegar. Negotiations start long before the formal negations begin. If you have developed a good relationship with your union leaders, you will know the hot button items and will be working on solutions that will profit the company and benefit the employees. Use the more positive approach before you become formal adversaries at the bargaining table. At that point, the attitudes shift,

and the rules change. You will find you are just the cut-man while the fight rages in the ring.

7. Take another bite at the apple as soon as possible. Ask for a one-year contract. Unions want contracts that last three to five years, thus guaranteeing a continuation of their dues. Management on the other hand will want—or should want—the opportunity to slice the pie again. Business is constantly evolving, and a one-year contract is really the only practical way to address these alterations in processes and business climate. Be aware that your labor relations people will advise against a one-year contract. Like the union, they want a three- to five-year contract. Do you want to know why? They view a one-year contract as too much work (they will never admit this as the reason), and they will make their case that a one-year contract exposes the company to greater odds for a strike based simply on the volume of the number of contract openings over a period. The real-world benefits will far outweigh this nebulous risk.

8. Separate the wheat from the chaff. Know the difference between the relatively valueless and items of true worth. We often make the mistake of digging in our heels over things that have emotional value to us. We will sacrifice or minimize the things that are truly of value in order to get these nuggets of fool's gold.

9. Only the strong survive. One of the union's tactics is simply to wear you down. Multiple days of late-night negotiations are designed to make you fatigued, causing you to be more likely to give in to their demands or make a blundering mental error. Learn to take it easy while playing the game. Recognize it for what it is. Remain in control at all

times, and if you feel yourself slipping, call a time-out for some nutrition and sleep. If you play it right, you can turn the game on them, causing them to agree to items that you would not have thought possible. During negotiations some years ago, around four AM, a plant manager complained to me about the negotiations running into the early morning hours. I told him that if he wanted a lesson in negotiations, he should watch *The Hustler*, especially the part where Minnesota Fats, after playing for twenty-five straight hours, freshens up, combs his hair, powders his hands, puts a fresh flower in his label, and says to Eddie Felson, "Fast Eddie, let's play some pool." (Fast-forward five years. I had received a promotion at work. The above plant manager, whom I had not seen or spoken to since the negotiations, sent me an email containing only this line—"Fast Eddie, let's play some pool!" He had not forgotten the lesson.) This is where the rubber meets the road. People who are not willing to run marathons should try out for the water polo team.

Lesson from the Ranch

Sometimes you get what you deserve.

119

CHAPTER

20

Leadership

"So ignore them. They are blind guides leading the blind, and if one blind
person guides another, they will both fall into a ditch."
Matthew 15:14

"If you're ridin' ahead of the herd, take a look back every now and then
to make sure it's still there."
Cowboy Wisdom

What does it take to get five thousand head of cattle across open rangeland from San Antonio to Abilene? How do you patrol and control five hundred square miles of pasture? How do you get men to sleep on the hard ground, bust their tails from sun up to sun down, brand cattle, and birth calves on the outskirts of civilization? Why does your team rally when it experiences floods, disease, insects, freezing cold, and blistering heat? When the drought is so bad, the trees are bribing the dogs? Without even mentioning the rattlesnakes and gopher holes? How do you accomplish all of this, and at the end of the day, have people who are bursting with pride?

You do it through leadership. Great leadership is as natural to ranch life as tall grass and clear water. Like most natural things, you don't tend to notice and appreciate leadership until it is missing. Even though a rancher is a great leader, he may not be regarded as such. His people think they did it all by themselves. That's why he is great instead of only good.

I have studied this a great deal, and I have concluded that great leaders are born that way. They have a spark in them that fires differently from your average person. I think, too, that the great leaders never seek the job; the job seeks them. If someone wants to be my leader, advises me of such, and then goes about the task of trying to lead me, there is a good chance he will be seeing my backside very soon. I will balk on him like an overheated mule. I bet you would do the same.

Now, I believe you can teach the attributes of leadership, and if given enough time and patience along with a good mentor, someone can become a good leader. I will take a good leader any day over the hordes of mediocre and poor leaders that our businesses now produce. We have lost sight of the fact that a leader serves his followers and is not in the game for his own personal enrichment. How sad it is to see the majority of people having to suffer at work due to a poor leader. We never correct this because we have lost the ability to weed out the poor leaders. Many of us confuse a good administrator with a good leader. The administrator is very competent in compiling and adhering to policies and rules, but he doesn't have a clue how to lead people. Often, a good person can be a good leader with only limited attributes. H.G. Wells said, "In the Country of the Blind, the one-eyed Man is King."

One of the most important jobs of a manager is to stay out of the way of the born leader. Next on the list would be to mold the administrators into good leaders: not an easy task for most managers, as most are administrators themselves. The human resources field is not usually a natural draw for leaders. I wish it were not true, but it is. Sometimes great leaders emerge, but not often enough. Most people wind up in human resources because they have excellent administrative and clerical skills. Human resources is also a place where the mathematically challenged seem to end up. A few promotions later, they find they have the title of manager and don't really know what to do with it except to keep right on doing what they have done in the past. They administer things to death, throw in a few big words, act important, and hope nobody finds out they are faking it.

Therefore, before we try to mold others into leaders, we need to take a long look in the mirror. Before you can teach bull riding, you need to be able to stay on for eight seconds at least a few times.

I line my bookshelf with leadership books. It contains big books, skinny books, and all sizes in between. They all contain well-meaning advice. Some disagree with others, and others disagree with all, but largely, they are all good books. Leadership has always intrigued me, so I want to know as much as I can about the subject. I have always struggled to define leadership. If you ask ten people, you'll get ten different answers. One person whom I asked defined leadership as providing guidance and direction. I asked him if a road map qualified as a leader. He scratched his head as he walked off. Well, I still cannot define leadership, but like the world's biggest horse, I know it when I see it.

In 2004, the United States War College studied its major generals in Iraq. They asked subordinates to anonymously rate their leaders. From this survey, they developed a list of "The Big 12" leadership attributes. To date, it is the best-published information I have encountered on leadership.

You can Google it by typing in *Leadership Lessons at Division Command Level.* Working with managers and continuous improvement gurus to incorporate the essence of this report into various leadership courses, we have tweaked it, massaged it, revised, deleted, and added to it. Using the War College report as a basis, I believe we can now define the attributes of leadership from a business perceptive. I use them as my benchmarks as I learn to be a better leader. In order of importance, the attributes are as follows:

- **Composed under Stress.** This attribute can also be seen as the stability of the mind under pressure. When trouble rains down and the world as we know it ceases to exist, what better place to run for cover than the person who has the ability to remain calm as chaos erupts? This doesn't mean the person doesn't care or lacks a sense of urgency. It simply means he can keep his head on while others are losing theirs. This is a rare trait indeed. Edmund Burke said, "No passion so effectually robs the mind of all its powers of acting and reasoning as fear."

- **Broad Perspective.** This is the ability to combine context and perspective. Being able to grasp both the individual situation and the environmental factors surrounding it is essential to success. A so-called leader mired in the mud is doing a disservice to his followers. Having the ability to rise above it all and base his leadership on the totality of circumstances both seen and unseen is the hallmark of a great leader. (See chapter on the Big Picture.)

- **Difficult Choices.** Someone has to step up to the plate and call the shots that will anger people. It may be as simple as terminating an underperformer or as complex as permanently closing a facility. Whether the decision is simple or complex, great leaders will move forward on a timely basis and make the difficult decision. They don't enjoy it. Nevertheless, they recognize it, swallow their fear, and make the best choices for everyone involved. They understand that others may criticize their choices, but they move forward anyway. (See chapter on decisions.)

- **Communicates Effectively**. After successfully ruling the Earth for 250,000 years, the Neanderthals disappeared. The theories of this disappearance range from murder by modern man to starvation due to competition with modern man to inbreeding with the new kids on the block. Regardless of the various theories, all scientists agree that the Neanderthals' weak communication skills were their downfall. Without excellent language skills, they were not able to plan, organize, and lead. They could not respond to the new challenges. If would-be leaders don't want to put in the time and effort to communicate effectively , they should remember the Neanderthal. Have you seen any lately? I mean, besides your wife's relatives.

Although I wrote this book primarily as a management guide, other chapters in this book deal with subjects which are also leadership attributes. Two such chapters are the ones on ethics and dealing with bad news.

Teaching someone to be a great leader is not possible. However, teaching someone to be a good leader is. We too often focus our education and training on the competencies of the job as defined by technical skills, process analysis, reporting. We focus on these areas because it is easy, and we can see instant results. As our obsession with fast food and instant messaging illustrates, we don't like to wait. However, leadership takes more time, and we can fully never understand it. That doesn't mean we should not be constantly pushing the leadership principles. We should teach and instruct as often as realistically possible. Even though we may believe we are just wasting our time, we will be pleasantly surprised when we realize how much of our teachings has been absorbed. Of course, the best way to groom new leaders is to let them work under great or good leaders. The fortunate people find themselves under the wing of a great leader. This is something that mere money cannot buy.

As a pet peeve, it irritates me when I read about someone who is the *recognized leader* of [insert subject]. I don't know about you, but I never *recognize* the people who, I suspect, anointed themselves the *recognized leaders*. I wouldn't know them from Adam. I may have been working in that particular field for decades, but I never heard of them. I wish people would avoid this phrase unless they are talking about someone such as George Bush or Madonna, people I actually can recognize. It is just annoying, and I needed to get it off my chest.

I still don't know how to define leadership (and maybe I never will), but I have a good clue as to how to recognize when the teacher has achieved his goal. It is simple, really. The leader's followers are all winners.

Please understand that leadership and management are not the same. When the planets align and the two come together, it can be a wonderful event. Unfortunately, this is a rarity rather than the norm. In general, when I think of management—myself included—I think of the old ranch tale about the cowboy and the bull. Leading a Brahman bull into a restaurant around ten AM, a cowboy sits down and orders coffee. After finishing the cup, he draws his six-gun, kills the bull with a single shot between the eyes, and leaves. The next morning, he returns with another bull and asks for coffee again. "We're still cleaning up from yesterday," the waiter replies. "What was that about?" Smiling very big, the cowboy says, "I'm training for upper management. I come in late, drink coffee, shoot the bull, leave a mess for others to clean up, and disappear for the rest of the day."

Do you work with people like this, or do you work with leaders? It is a good question to ask. You will be spending roughly a third of your working life working with either leaders or bull shooters. How do you want to spend your valued time? The choice is always yours.

Lesson from the Ranch

A picture of a Texas sunset can be pretty but it doesn't compare to the real thing. Always look for natural leaders.

CHAPTER 21

Meetings

"On the first day of the week, we gathered with the local believers to share in the Lord's Supper."
Acts 20:7

"If it don't seem like it's worth the effort, it probably ain't."
Cowboy Wisdom

Most meetings that occur on the ranch are not unlike the meetings we should be having at work: spur-of-the-moment, spontaneous mini-meetings that are held at the corral, in the hay field, or late in the evening on the front porch. In the corporate world, the best meetings are held in individual offices, commons, hallways, and parking lots.

It is actually a rare occurrence when we absolutely need to meet. Even the Bible doesn't ask us to meet more than once a week, and that weekly meeting is regarding the fate of our eternal soul. Why should we meet more than once a week regarding the fate of our widgets?

As you know, most meetings are a waste of valuable time. Sometimes meetings are actually constructive; but a truly beneficial meeting is about as rare as hen's teeth. So why do we have so many of the blasted things? I believe most meetings fall into one of the following chutes:

- **Tradition Meetings**. Meetings are often just a practice of long standing. The company has been having the [insert name] meeting on a specific calendar day for so long that it is never questioned if it is really needed. These traditional meetings will be passed from manager to manager through the years. The meetings have been carved in stone so long that nobody remembers who started them, and certainly nobody wants to be the one to suggest they stop. *Suggestion:* Have a secret ballot vote to see if this meeting is worthwhile and should be continued.

- **Blame-sharing Meetings**. Many meetings are held because someone wants to pass the buck. A tough decision must be made, and the so-called leader can't or won't do it. So the leader calls a group together and hopefully somebody with a spinal column will step forward and suggest the needed action. All of a sudden, the leader is off the hook, and the forthcoming fallout can be shared by all. *Suggestion:* Recognize the meeting for what it is, but don't let the leader off the hook. Sometimes this is not realistic, but you should call him on it anyway. I have heard it said that sunlight is the best disinfectant.

- **Ego Fix Meetings**. Some people just need to have their egos stroked every so often, and what better way than to have a meeting of subordinates who will grovel in their presence? Poor or mediocre leaders yearn constantly for everyone to know just how important they are. What better way than to assemble the downtrodden and allow them to bask in the leader's glory? *Suggestion:* Slip this book under his door with a paper clip on this page.

- **Communication Meetings**. Information clearly needs to be shared within an organization, but does sharing the info really require a meeting? I recommend a meeting only if the information is of such a complex nature that it will take a lengthy Q-and-A period to understand the message.

- **Free Lunch Meetings**. They say there is no such thing as a 'free lunch.' There is if it's put on an expense account. What percentage of lunch meetings result in sincere productive work versus the percentage that result in a really good fajita with chips and salsa? *Suggestion:* Cut this farce out. If you want to have lunch, then go to lunch. Stop winking at everyone and calling it work. You can put your cowboy boots in the oven but that still don't make 'em biscuits.

- **Planning or Project-driven Meetings**. Ah, finally we really have a reason for meeting. Even so, this type of meeting should be short and to the point. After the project or plan is implemented, meet only as needed for follow-up and feedback. A proper meeting must be led by an agenda, oriented by a written action plan, and followed by minutes (one page) issued the same day. The rule is that the meeting starts on time even if everyone is not there, and ends on time, if not before. We tend to sit around and wait for the late attendees (see "village idiot" below) before we start our meetings, which puts everyone in a foul mood to start with. If you start on time regardless, you'll note a great improvement in punctuality. At the end of the meeting, all in attendance know the roles they will be playing and have actual plans to put into effect when they leave the room.

Now that we have the meeting types identified, let's take a close look at the meeting attendees:

1. The facilitator or leader. This is the person who has called the meeting (or allowed it to continue) and who may or may not be in control of the agenda. *Suggestion:* For Christmas or his birthday, pool your money and get him *The Complete Idiot's Guide to Meeting and Event Planning* (Amazon.com, $14.16).

2. Forty percent don't need to be at the meeting because they have no input or the subject is over their heads. Sometimes this sub-group attends because they have nothing else to do and need to look busy. *Suggestion:* This is a hard one to solve, but I recommend not inviting them.

3. Another forty percent actually need to be at the meeting, but are distracted by the leader's tangents, digression, and general ill-preparedness. They leave the meeting not only having gained nothing but also having lost an hour. This is a really sad group, because they are the ones who are really running the organization and making a profit (or not) for everyone else. *Suggestion:* They meet alone. Cut all the others out of the loop. They will be happy, and the company will be more likely to make money.

4. Ten percent are the village idiots. They are only there to show up late, disrupt, ensure digression, ridicule, polish their comedic skills, and generally upset the other eighty percent, thus ensuring that the facilitator will have to call another meeting where, once again, nothing will be accomplished. *Suggestion:* Give them something shiny to play with at the meeting. If this doesn't work, then, by hint or force, they need to be relocated to another village.

5. Ten percent—the balance—feel they are just a little smarter than everyone else. They are not interested in any ideas except their own. You get the feeling that the other attendees are really just taking up space in the room as this ten percent proceeds to let you know how superior they are to you and everyone else. *Suggestion:* Stick to the agenda and the action plan to see how much these peacocks actually produce. This will force them to work instead of preen. *Another suggestion:* Pick out the know-it-alls and put them in a "special" meeting by themselves. This 'special' meeting will be confidential (they like this word) so the other buffoons won't be involved. The buffoons can then have their meeting and get some actual work done.

Lesson from the Ranch

When it concerns meetings, when in doubt, don't.

133

Mission Statements

"When people do not accept divine guidance, they run wild.
But whoever obeys the law is joyful."
Proverbs 29:18

"The best sermons are lived, not preached."
Cowboy Wisdom

Take out a piece of paper and quickly write down the mission or vision statement from the last three organizations for which you worked, including your current employer. Can you do it? Don't feel bad, neither can I. Nevertheless, I can tell you what the unwritten mission statement was at every place I ever worked. It was: To make money. There is nothing wrong with that mission. It is a perfectly decent and honest statement. That is why we are here. The corporation makes money, the stockholders make money, the employees make money, and the government makes money. It is all about the money. However, this sounds a little harsh and brutal and doesn't give us a warm, fuzzy feeling, so we formulate a mission statement layered in moralistic and high-minded elements, shoehorning in words such as world class, leader, service, quality, safety.

I once spent three cold, wintry days in the Midwest working with a mission statement team. We were constructing the 'much-needed' mission statement for the corporate human resources group. Eight hours a day for three days of stringing words together and debating things, including comma placement (I am very serious). On the final day, the executive in charge of the production side of business attended our session and offered his unsolicited advice. Because he outranked everyone in the room, we threw away two days of work and started afresh. How foolish was this? The only positive aspect of the entire trip was the superior quality of Midwestern porterhouse steaks.

For me, it seems awful pompous of us to think that every for-profit organization is so unique and special that each one needs its own unique and special mission statement. It is so pretentious it's painful to watch. Could you imagine the look on a trail boss's face if you asked him for his mission statement prior to a trail drive? He might say, "What part of 'sell these cattle in Omaha' do you not understand?" I cannot help but laugh when I visualize cowboys sitting around a campfire developing a mission statement.

Everything within an organization evolves. Processes change, customers change, management and leaders change, owners change. How can a mission statement realistically encapsulate all this evolution without being so nebulous as to be worthless?

In case you are wondering, the mission statement on my ranch is this: *Make Money / Have Fun.* If this is not the mission, then why in the world am I doing it? All of the adjectives and descriptors that could be included in a mission statement I choose to simply call *life.*

Lesson from the Ranch

Keep it simple.

23

Money

"Those who love money will never have enough. How meaningless to think that wealth brings true happiness!"
Ecclesiastes 5:10

"The quickest way to double your money is to fold it over and put it back into your pocket."
Cowboy Wisdom

The essayist and poet Ralph Waldo Emerson said, "Money often costs too much." That pretty much sums up the theme of this chapter. Money is an odd thing. It can bring freedom and leisure and allow you to sleep at night. On the other hand, money can make you lie, cheat, steal, and stay up all night long. It is not so much money itself and the amount of it you possess; it is a matter of how you perceive and manage money.

Looking back on my early childhood, I realize now that we were poor. As my parents struggled to establish their ranch, Dad worked at a low-income job so we could have the basics in life. The basics did not include indoor plumbing. Our outhouse was a fancy two-holer and the envy of our neighbors. (I never understood the need for two holes as nobody ever sat together that I recall.) We ordered our school clothes once a year from Sears and Roebuck. It was a good day when the clothes package arrived in the mail. It was a great day when they actually fit. During the summer, we wore cut-off jeans and went bare-chested and bare-footed. Except for staples such as salt and flour, all of our food came from the farm. We processed our own pork, milked our cow, collected eggs, and canned our vegetables. If I wanted to buy something in town, I had to work for the money. Only later in life did I find out that some kids got what they called an "allowance." I never could grasp the concept of getting money for nothing and still can't.

We were poor by the standards of the economy, but our clothes were clean, our teeth were brushed, and our bellies were full. My parents never struggled with paying the bills simply because they lived within their means. I remember them splurging one time and getting a television. I could have lived without Tom Terrific and his wonder dog, the mighty Manfred, but it sure was fun to watch. We had no lack of toys. I tied sewing thread to a June bug's leg and flew him around. I spent hours damming up creeks and ditches just to watch them wash away with the next heavy rain. Did you know that you could take a metal barrel hoop and a stick and spend days going up and down the road seeing how far you could roll the hoop without it falling over? We made marbles with red clay rolled into balls and sun-baked on a hot tin roof. A forked branch and a piece of inner tube made a dangerous weapon putting all squirrels and rabbits on notice; not that I ever killed one. I was just always a major threat with my noise and dust.

I know it sounds like a cliché, but there was a tremendous amount of love and laughter in our home. I wish I could join the rest of society and complain about my dysfunctional family, but I simply can't. We were poor as far as material possessions go, but we were rich in spirit, mind, and good health. Twisting the words of Emerson, money on the ranch did not 'cost much.'

One of the main things I tell people who are striving to advance in their career is this: don't chase money. I have seen this mistake happen numerous times, and the person always fails when salary, bonuses, rewards, become his or her driving goal. Instead, I advise people to chase excellence. If they do that, the money will naturally follow. Whether you are a clerk at a gas station or the manager of an advertising firm, if you work hard every day to be the best at your job and settle for nothing short of excellence in yourself and others, it won't be long before you are in the highly compensated crowd. It is a surefire formula for success.

Twice in my life, I have voluntarily accepted a move in my career for less money. Once was because I wanted to move from the production world into the human resources arena. I lost a large part of my weekly income. Since then, my salary has quadrupled, and I am now in an area where I can pursue excellence. You may ask why I couldn't have pursued excellence in manufacturing. The truth is, if you don't have a strong passion and enthusiasm for the field, you will forever find yourself believing that the status quo is good enough.

The other time I moved for less money we have discussed elsewhere in this book. Suffice it to say at this point, I left the company for less money because my values and the company's values did not align. That's not to say that I was right and they were wrong. I hope that I will never be pompous enough to think that I am always right and everyone else is a buffoon. I know better. I do know what values I personally hold dear, and I have just enough sense to know when these are threatened. My mind and body are not worth a few dollars a year. Never have been. Never will be.

Stick to your values and seek excellence. The money will be your dessert at the end of a good meal.

Lesson from the Ranch

Never chase money. Chase being the best and the money will show up like bees to honey.

CHAPTER 24

Organizational Charts

"No one can serve two masters. For you will hate one and love the other, you will be devoted to one and despise the other. You cannot serve both God and money."
Matthew 6:24

"If you get to thinkin' you're a person of influence, try orderin' somebody else's dog around."
Cowboy Wisdom

On the ranch, we don't have an organizational chart. If we did, I would be in the top box (see chapter on the Big Picture), and everyone else would be a straight horizontal line of boxes with no one reporting to anyone else.

If I were to operate by the business model of hierarchical management, with layers of VPs, each with their own assistants, things would slowly come to a complete halt. Even in my top dog position, my family will occasionally drag me off my high horse and force me to get in line with the rest of the family. This is the way it should be. Over time, everyone gravitates and dominates the areas where their personal strength lies. My son Jeremiah likes tactical planning and is the detail-oriented person . He also makes sure we get the best deals on equipment and supplies. Josh, my son-in-law, is a smart problem-solver with a strong mechanical aptitude. He has gotten us out of many binds. My wife Jan thrives on detail and is good with the books. She is excellent at making sure I don't lose touch with reality. Ginger, my daughter, is the one who keeps me truly grounded by her attitude toward life. She doesn't know it, but I am proud of her approach to life's ups and down. I wish I were more like her. My strength is sitting on the tailgate, drinking cold beer and discussing my aches and pains with anyone within earshot.

Alas, with companies, organizational charts don't follow the above pattern. Instead of King Arthur and his Knights of the Round Table (the world's best organizational chart), we have developed a system in which everyone in authority is graded, ranked, and placed above his or her subordinates and below his or her superiors. Even organized religion, the Mafia, and street gangs use organizational charts, if not on paper, then at least in practice. I have found that the higher up people are in the organizational chart, the more they want to see periodic updates and find inventive uses for organizational charts in their decision-making processes. Conversely, lower-ranking people don't tend to find much use for organizational charts and certainly don't want or need the periodic updates.

Nobody wants to be below someone else. Most people want to be partners in an enterprise.. However, some people in the top boxes like to see the structure laid out in this manner. It supports their narcissistic nature and balloons their self-importance. I have even seen organizational charts being distributed on the Internet and, in one case, actually posted on hallway bulletin boards. Of course, many are so low on the food chain that they don't even make the chart. Since only a few can sit at the top, our serfdom system demoralizes most people. Is this the way we inspire?

When newly hired people start on the job, many companies will give them an organizational chart, so they will know who reports to whom in the individual departments. As a practical concern, the company will point out the low-hanging box that the new hire has just filled. This is just another way of saying, "In the scheme of things, you matter very little." If you'll observe, the people who implement this practice or allow it to exist are always at or close to the top of the pyramid. What's the best way to find out who's who in an organization? May I suggest foot leather? The newly hired person needs to spend a good portion of his or her first couple of weeks just visiting with different departments and really getting to know his or her coworkers. Alternatively, as they say on the ranch, "We've howdied, but we ain't shook yet."

Another train wreck that we have created in our reporting structures is the infamous *dotted line*. This is where you report directly to the head of the department, but you also report (to a lesser degree) to someone actually at the location or vice versa. This is an unfair situation for all parties con-cerned. It tends to confuse and sometimes bewilder. I have seen situations in the past where the two top boxes were fighting over control of the subordinate. I have also seen cases where the subordinate played both superiors against each other, resulting in animosity and a halt to productivity. Oh, the games we play. I believe I reached the height of foolishness when I worked for a company that actually had obtained software that would shorten or lengthen the distance between the dashes in the dotted line indicating the *strength of relation-ship*. Supposedly, a formal Causal Association Analysis deter-mines this. Take the inventors of this process and send them to the night shift, where they can kick rocks and count stars. They still won't make you money, but at least they will have been quarantined so they won't infect the organization with their dim-witted ideas.

Organizational charts have a useful existence in the following limited scope:

1. **Planning tool**. A special one-time workforce-modeling tool primarily used in mergers or downsizing.

2. **Affirmative action review**. This we incorporate with #3.

3. **EEO Tracking**. This is a good tool for maintaining continuous tracking for ethnicity, sex, tenure, and salary. An organization with a multitude of organizational charts needs this managerial tool to maintain balance and fairness.

4. **Job openings**, especially in a large organization. An organizational chart is sometimes useful, but even then, this function also can be combined with #3.

Here are some suggestions you might want to adopt:

1. If you currently post your organizational charts, remove them immediately.

2. If your organization uses cute, different-shaped boxes differentiating executives from managers from grunts, just stop it or move to a country where class matters.

3. Decide who should report to whom and remove those silly dotted lines. For help, see the chapter on decisions.

4. Maintain *confidential* organizational charts only within human resources, and never distribute them.

5. Put your best and brightest minds to work on how to eliminate organizational charts altogether.

When I was twelve years old, I got my first paying job at a chicken hatchery. My dad worked there, hauling baby chicks out to the farms, to supplement the cattle and eventually pay off the ranch note. I would go by after school and work until dark, when Mom or Dad would pick me up. I don't remember the pay, but it was a great deal of money for a twelve-year-old kid. I bought the most expensive harmonica in town with my first check. I still have it. It cost so much that I was afraid to play it, so it is still brand-new. When school was out in the summer, I worked at the hatchery full time. I learned every job in the place. I excelled at some and was horrid at others, but in the end, it all balanced out. It was a great place to work, and we had a ton of fun. We also had the highest hatchability and livability, not only in the company but in the nation. We didn't achieve this record every year I worked there, but most years we did. However, don't think I'm trying to tell you this success was due to me. They would have done even better if they didn't have to spend time correcting my blunders.

As time went by and I learned about other industries and organizations, one thing about the hatchery began to stand out. There were no bosses. Oh, there was one person who called himself the assistant manager, but he never told anyone what to do, and I am sure no one would have listened if he did. He was an older fellow who spent most of his time talking to the young girls. Everyone laughed him off, back then. Of course, today it would be called sexual harassment. The so-called hatchery manager was also the breeder manager and spent ninety-five percent of his time on the breeder farms. My dad ran his own show. The vaccination crew did their

147

thing. The maintenance people were very self-directed. The egg setters and transfer crew were without bosses: when problems arose, they handled them themselves. The tray wash man was lord of his domain and was quick to tell you he did his own thing. The nephew of the hatchery manager did designate himself as *lead*; however, he worked alone so I don't know what he was leading.

I can't recall a single time that anyone missed work. No one was ever late for work. If there were ice or snow on the roads, the ones with trucks or jeeps would go around picking everyone up. It wasn't a decision; it was just done. The hatchery manager would stop by every other day just to see if someone needed something, and then he would be on his way. Everyone had great pride in the hatchery ranking.

We were some of the lowest paid people in town. Farm-type labor always is. Since we worked in farm-classified jobs, we weren't even eligible for overtime. Nevertheless, I never heard anyone complain about the pay or hours of work. I also saw little turnover. Everyone knew exactly what percentage the hatch was running and which competitor might be closing in on us.

One team, no boss, goal-oriented, pride in workmanship. I sometimes wonder how bad I could have messed them up with Causal Association Analysis and an organizational chart.

Lesson from the Ranch

Use organizational charts like you use whiskey: only in moderation and keep it away from buffoons.

CHAPTER 25

Pride

"Pride leads to disgrace, but with humility comes wisdom."
Proverbs 11:2

"Don't swagger around the ranch in your Stetson and Tony Lamas when your wife has to work in town."
Cowboy Wisdom

I have to admit that writing this chapter was personally painful. Of all of my sins and vices, I know beyond a shadow of doubt that pride is my worst offense. Those who don't agree with my self-assessment have only to ask my wife. In her wisdom, she has been trying for years to tone down my pride and increase my humility. She hasn't been very successful. As I've tried to explain to her, my pride and arrogance are what pays the bills. Without these attributes, I wouldn't have the confidence to excel at my profession.

149

Truthfully, I know as well as she does that this is all bull butter. I only use this as an excuse because, like other addictions, I have a hard time giving it up. I dream up excuses for my prideful ways. In my heart, I know the evils of pride, and I know the many ways it has harmed me in the past. Yet I resist humility as if it were a weakness rather than the strength it truly is. Therefore, this chapter is as much self-reflection as it is counsel and recommendations. Maybe you can learn from my stubbornness. Moreover, like a hellfire and brimstone preacher, I just might step on your toes, too. If you find that I am hitting too close to home, if you strongly disagree and this angers you, then you need to read the chapter twice—slowly.

Years ago, we bought a fine stallion to assist us on the ranch. He was the most handsome horse I had ever seen. He held his head erect, nose in the air, and had a jaunty jig to his step. He was the best of the best, and he knew it. There is nothing wrong with that. There is nothing better in this world than to sit aside a fine horse as you work the cattle herd; that is, unless the fine stallion comes to you dragging a sled full of pride. This particular horse knew that he was superior to everything else in the pasture. His haughty attitude toward the other animals and especially toward us simple humans became a real problem very fast. To ride or not to ride was a decision he made, not you. His harassment of the other animals not only resulted in upsetting the natural order of things but also occasionally resulted in actual injury to the livestock.

Not having the time, patience, or knowledge about how to correct prideful behavior (where is a horse whisperer when you need one?), we sold the stallion to another ranch. We had learned our lesson at the expense of only one broken collarbone and a few head of battered and bruised livestock.

His new owner, being wiser than we were, castrated him the first day. That was the stallion's reward for his past deeds. After healing up, this horse and his newfound attitude became an excellent addition to the man's ranch. The rancher was happy, and so was the horse. I am certainly not advocating this operation for mankind, but pride will eventually catch up to us and lead to our destruction.

So how do we keep from being 'castrated' by pride? (Shocked by my metaphors? Remember, this book is is par of the *Lessons from the Ranch* series.) First off, let us define what we mean by pride. There could be some confusion on this point, so clarification is in order. The pride we are discussing here is not to be confused with having self-respect and believing in your own value. We are also not concerned with having pride in our achievements or the achievements of others, such as being proud of our children's good grades in school. We are not even talking about our hatred of falling below our own standards, although this area is thin ice. While confidence and self-respect often wear the same clothes as arrogance, they are not to be confused with each other . They can appear the same from across the street. It is only when we stop to talk to them that we can detect the difference.

Our target is the pride exemplified by unreasonable and inordinate self-esteem. In today's society, pride is often seen as a minor vice at worst, or even a disputed 'virtue'. In Martha Stewart's words: "It's a good thing." Nothing could be further from the truth. When I start leaning toward agreeing with the masses and believing that pride is a trivial sin, I have only to remember that Satan's existence came about as a direct result of pride. The most evil vice we have is pride. All of the other vices are nothing compared to this hidden demon.

The distinction between the pride of self-respect and achievement and the pride of inordinate self-esteem is easily made. This latter form of pride equates to vainglory. Years ago, vainglory was a very horrible, diabolical thing to possess. That term has fallen out of use in the current day as our morals have loosened. Nowadays, people such as Donald Trump are the standard we aspire to. This is how far we have fallen and lost our bearing.

151

In Jim Collins' excellent book *Good to Great*, one thing that surprised me was his discovery that the most effective leaders of industry were also the most humble. This was a shock for me, as I had always wrongly considered all top executives to be prideful and boastful. After reading this book, I started comparing the long-term performance of various companies with their leadership. Jim Collins was right on point. The companies that had 'flashy' leaders would do well for a while, but eventually they would fall from grace. The organizations that had humble leaders consistently turned a profit and grew. When I reviewed my own past employers, the successful companies were the ones with humble leaders at the helm. Over time, the 'peacock' leaders either destroyed the company or greatly reduced its size.

At the heart of pride is competition. Remember that Competition's twin brother is Rivalry, and they both hate their next-door neighbor, Friendship. Let's see if we can prove this point. Do you know someone who is proud of his automobile, his home, or his good looks? He is not proud of these achievements so much as he is proud that his car is better than yours is, his house is bigger than yours is, and he attracts the opposite sex more than you. Success in the rivalry makes him proud. He has beaten the enemy (you) good and solid. If you remove the competition, you remove the pride. Take away the opposition, and you will eliminate the conceit.

I, too, love competition, and to some extent, competition within an organization can be a good thing. However, there is a world of difference between friendly contests and the sort of competition that is pride-driven. The first adds some salt to life. The other is pure hostility.

Why does a man or woman who has risen to the level of vice president of XYZ Company spend so much time and energy trying to rise to the senior vice president position? Surely, he or she has enough money. I will agree that there are people who seek higher office because they truly believe they can benefit more people or because they are simply being under-utilized. Unfortunately, most people out there have other motives. Is it because someone out there has more power? Some misguided people feel the need to be superior over the largest number of people possible. This is true in industry, organized religion, and politics. In fact, I suspect that it is not only superiority they pursue, but also feeling so superior to other mere mortals that they don't have to care what others think of them, just as long as they do their bidding. Do you know anyone like this? If you don't, it could be you. My theory is that these prideful people will rise to the top, yet their stay is always brief. When they arrive, their suitcase contains only pride. They forgot all the important things, including humility.

What does all of this mean to you and me? Before we move on to the meat of this chapter, I would like to point out that we must always be on high alert and resist hiring the person who fits the above description of pride. By its nature, a résumé is a bragging document. Since you are presenting to the world a picture of you, typed on a white sheet of paper, you would naturally want to present a picture of achievement and confidence. As often as not, we stretch and mold these achievements to present the best portrait possible, buoyed by semi-facts. Indeed, in our darkest moments, we boldly fabricate facts. That is why we cannot rely on résumés to tell us anything about a person other than he or she appears to be qualified for the position through education, experience, or a combination of both. During the face-to-face interview process, it would be wise to explore these achievements and other areas of interest a person might have, just to see if you get a humble or prideful response. My suggestion would be to do this until you are satisfied that you know the truth. If you are not sure, it is better to bring an applicant back for additional interviews with you and others. Bringing someone into your organization who believes pride is a virtue is one of the most egregious things you can do as a management professional. The diabolical pride that you allowed in the door is a cancer. It can destroy the entire organization. (See the chapter on connected.) It is critical to remember that every person in our organization carries varying degrees of both good and evil in his heart. Our task is to attempt to determine the degree and make decisions accordingly.

Now, we are ready for the main purpose of this chapter. Of all the different positions within the organization, where pride is concerned, human resources is the most important. The reasons are evident. In our position, we have major influence on the people we select to join or leave our team. We are the gatekeepers.

Do we use an unassuming nature when dealing with conflict and discipline and the general administration of our policies, or do we perform these tasks from a position of arrogance, conceit, and self-importance? Are we actually building our organization one person at a time, or do we—unconsciously—aim for its destruction? If we wish to be the very best we can be, it is vital to hold up a mirror and take a cold, objective look. As C.S. Lewis wrote, "If you think you are not conceited, it means you are very conceited indeed." Now where did I put that mirror?

Many moons ago, when my daughter Ginger was in her teens, she was on the high school drill team. I was very proud of her. Here I was, the father of a drill team member. It seemed that most of the drill team members' parents were well-to-do; therefore, my family must be climbing up the social ladder.

The time came for the annual drill team tryouts. Even after a girl was already on the team, she still had to try out for the next year's squad. Ginger's confidence was high, but she still practiced diligently to ensure her skills would be sharp for the upcoming trials. On tryout day, I have to admit I was a little nervous.

Ginger didn't make the team. For whatever reason, the committee decided to choose someone else. While I hid my anger, I was upset. I started thinking bad thoughts about the committee, the school, the snotty, well-to-do parents, and everything else associated with this 'joke.' I swore I would never have anything to do with this stupid school again. In fact, in my mind, I was plotting against the committee members. I wanted revenge.

Greater than my anger was my fear that Ginger had been hurt in the process. If it affected me this strongly, I could only imagine how upset she must be. This was my little baby girl, and I was supposed to protect her from the world.

A few days later, I asked Janita where Ginger had disappeared to. She said Ginger was visiting a friend. As it turned out, one of the girls who would be trying out for the junior high drill team had asked Ginger to tutor her in the steps and nuances of the routines. Ginger had readily agreed and had been working with this girl for several days. At the junior high tryouts, the girl performed flawlessly; and she was among the announced winners.

Instead of taking the rejection as a negative, Ginger had reached out in a positive way to tutor a young person. Instead of sulking and thinking depressing thoughts, Ginger had put on a smile and diverted her energy into the very field that had rejected her.

I pondered on this for a short time, and then I experienced an epiphany. In a flash, I realized how very wrong I had been and how very right Ginger had been. I had allowed pride to control me. Ginger, being a better person than me, had not allowed pride to affect her. With her attitude and actions, she had taken pride head on and defeated it. I was prouder of her for this than if she had been on ten drill teams. In the final analysis, the drill team was a minor item. The way she had handled a setback was of major importance. It revealed her true essence: the kind of person she was, and the kind of adult she would become.

To this day, when I recognize pride seeping in, I recall Ginger's teenage trial and draw wisdom from my daughter. I am not always successful, but I am trying.

Lesson from the Ranch

Your worst enemy is revealed each time you pass a mirror. Corral the beast within.

CHAPTER 26

Racial Discrimination

*"There is no longer Jew or Gentile, slave or free, male and female.
For you are all one in Christ Jesus."*
Galatians 3:28

*"A man is weighed by the bond of his word, the grit in his craw and his
love of God, Family, and Country. Nothing else carries weight."*
Cowboy Wisdom

This chapter is a bit long simply because of the com
plexity of the issue. Part of the complexity lies with
he fact that most people don't see themselves as

having any racial bias. Here is a quick quiz. Who were the first two men to reach the summit of Mount Everest on May 29, 1953? (The answer is at the end of the chapter.)

From the end of the Civil War until the mid-1880s were the high times for American cowboys. Since that time, they have grown in legend and myth. Forty thousand cowboys worked the trail drives as they pushed cattle across the Great Plains. A lot of people view the old western cowboys of this era as looking like Roy Rogers. In fact, a wide spectrum of humanity comprised this fraternal order. Ex-Union soldiers who didn't want to return home and former Rebels looking for new homes and fast action rode side-by-side for the same brand. Europe contributed to the cowboy ranks by sending us the continent's destitute immigrants and an odd lot of Englishmen called *remittance men*, the ne'er-do-well offspring of titled English families.

One little-known aspect of this motley crew was its ethnic mix. One in seven cowboys was Mexican (*vaquero*). In fact, the *vaqueros* were the original cowboys. One in six cowboys was black. Most of the blacks had been slaves on Texas ranches. Once free, they had all the skills necessary for gainful employment on cattle drives, and could rope and ride with the best of them. (Read up on Nat Love. He was a young black man who joined a trail drive at fifteen and later became a rodeo celebrity.) Estimates vary, but many sources believe that Indians or whites who had Indian blood in them also made up at least one out of every six cowboys. Assuming these figures are reasonably accurate, that means roughly forty-nine percent of all American cowboys did not look like Roy Rogers. At the end of the drive, I am sure they all smelled like Trigger, but I digress. On the trail, character was the mark of a man. Banded together for months at a time, miles from civilization, people's moral and ethical actions and reactions were paramount. Every man had to pull his own weight and accept the direction and scorn of the uncompromising trail boss. Age, race, and background were insignificant. In today's world, the courts talk about a company creating a *hostile environment*. The cowboy's hostile environments included heatstroke and rattlesnakes in your bedroll. I am not trying to flower it up and claim that discrimination didn't exist on trail drives. I am confident that it did. However, during that short span of time, numerous stories rolled out of the plains. These tales were of heroism and cowardly acts. They spoke of colorful characters and desperados.

One of the more colorful characters of the Old West was United States Marshall Bass Reeves. Marshall Reeves was born in 1838 at Van Buren, Arkansas, and worked for "Hanging Judge" Isaac C. Parker in Fort Smith, Arkansas. During a thirty-two-year career, Reeves developed a reputation for having superior detective skills and being a crack shot with a pistol or rifle. Before he retired in 1907, Marshall Reeves had arrested more than four thousand felons. One time, he rode into Fort Smith with seventeen criminals in handcuffs following him into town. During his career, Reeves had to kill fourteen outlaws while making arrests. He was never shot; however, he did have his belt blasted off one time. Scholars consider Reeves to be one of the most outstanding frontier heroes in United States history. Bass Reeves was born a slave. Now that we know that the cowboy society was a racially diverse group, can you recall any recounting of racial discrimination or turmoil? Maybe there is a lesson here.

The point of the chapter is not to discuss the various federal and state laws that deal with race and national origin. You are already well versed in these. We are not going to discuss legal strategies or your organization's policies and training. Each organization is unique, and plans will and should vary. Of better use is to discuss the root – not historical — causes why racial discrimination and the perception of racial discrimination are still alive and well in the United States. Blacks, whites, and Hispanics are the main topics in this chapter (with a little Indian thrown in). I understand other races such as Asians and Arabs have discrimination issues, but compared to blacks and Hispanics, I don't believe Asians and Arabs affect our national well-being and our court systems to the extent of the black and Hispanic issues.

Why do we continue to have Americans with a dual moniker? Do we not know who we are? Why do the authorities persist in hyphenating Americans? Are the people who carry these hyphenated nametags the ones who perpetuate this practice? Whose idea is this, and who allows its existence? Do they somehow think this will make people feel better? The use of African-American, Asian-American, Jamaican-American, Mexican-American, is simply wrong.

Native American is another example of our divisive nature (whether intended or not). Back in the 1970s, some white do-gooder in government decided to refer to Indians as Native Americans. The government official meant this as a term of respect. They should have asked the Indians what they wanted instead of shoving a meaningless descriptor down their throats. Most Native Americans refer to themselves as Indians, so why not the rest of us? I have a better idea. How about we refer to everyone as Americans and stop all this confusion? Apparently, I don't have an original idea. President Theodore Roosevelt popularized the term "hyphenated American" in the 1910s. The following excerpt is from a speech he gave on October 12, 1915, to the Knights of Columbus: "...There is no such thing as a hyphenated American who is a good American. The only man who is a good American is the man who is an American and nothing else."

How sad. Almost hundred years later, we still don't get it.

National origin is closely associated with race. People can claim national origin discrimination due to a physical, cultural, or linguistic characteristic of a national group. The federal government validates national origin (and implicitly racial discrimination) claims based on the charging party's appearance, self-identification, or community recognition. Why in this so-called enlightened age do we still allow these identification pegholes to exist? I have worked with people from Pakistan, Vietnam, Japan, China, Mexico, Costa Rica, South Africa, and Kenya. No matter his or her national origin, every single person was a hard-working, productive American. While rightfully proud of their ancestors, they were Americans in the fullest sense. Why does the government continue to drive wedges between Americans? Is it self-serving? Does it keep the various agencies staffed and flush with tax dollars? Misguided, well-meaning people often don't realize the harm they are doing. Maybe it is simple fear. Is it fear of stepping up to the plate and taking on special interest groups?

The National Geographic Society has an ongoing DNA project. For a small fee, you can submit your DNA, and they will send you a detailed "map" of your origin and your ancestors' journey across the Earth. Based on the genetic evidence, each one of us is related to a common African ancestor. As our ancestors traveled the landscape, different groups chose to settle in a wide range of climates. These different climates gave us a wide array of colors and features. Even though eons have passed, the obvious genetic markers describe our travelogue. Therefore, scientifically, I can prove that any one of us has a country of origin other than the United States. What we are really dealing with is the time factor. How long of a time span do we need to justify a discrimination charge?

Hispanics are hard to pin down as a racial group. although the federal government demands that we do so. Cameron Diaz and Martin Sheen certainly look different from Sammy Sosa and Roberto Clemente; however, all four are Hispanic. I would never confuse Rita Hayworth with Fidel Castro, but both would check Hispanic on the application addendum. In addition, Hispanics come from twenty-four Latin American countries. Therefore, I can rule out appearance and cultural differences. That leaves us with only recognition as the determining factor.

Do we discriminate against Hispanics? In the past, we certainly did. Segregated within the border towns, Hispanic housing consisted largely of dilapidated shacks coupled with unpaved streets, poor sewage systems and weak education systems. Today, Hispanics have made great strides, but we can all do much better. Unlike the waves of European immigrants at the turn of the twentieth century, Hispanics are not too keen on cutting their cultural ties with their places of birth. In large part, this is due to simple geography. Unlike Europeans, who have to cross the Atlantic Ocean, most Hispanics can reach their former homes by car or a short flight. In fact, many can simply walk home. At celebrations or protests, Hispanics wave their ancestral flags. I am not a chest-pounding patriot, but this is simply wrong.

To compound this problem, Americans have an enormous interest in promoting multiculturalism and maintaining separate ethic identities. When the European immigrants came ashore, they adopted our civic values, cultural norms, even habits of dress and hygiene. Today, we are all about diversity, even to the point of celebrating Cinco de Mayo and excluding Independence Day: which gradually erodes our common identity as Americans. These multicultural policies extend into our voting ballots, job preferences, college admissions, every facet of our societal lives. We, as Americans, now encourage — with the force of law — groups of *other* Americans to divide themselves by ancestry. Whatever happened to *E pluribus unum*, one out of many?

The small town where I grew up now has a majority Hispanic population. While I was growing up there, there were no Hispanics. This change took place over the last fifteen to twenty years. I find it amazing that not a single person of Hispanic origin has ever run for any kind of local political office. Surely they could easily win the race, giving them a position of authority from which to enact change. I suggest that if an ethnic group wanted to assimilate into the fabric of American society, this would be the place to start: grass-roots, small-town America.

A hot topic across our nation is the question of illegal status regarding Hispanics. I am not smart enough to figure out the correct answer. However, as a first step, I would move the Statue of Liberty from New York to South Texas. I always thought that the strength and decency of America lay in our compassion and willing acceptance of people wanting a better life. What does the statue say? "Give me your tired, your poor, your huddled masses yearning to breathe free." Do we really mean this, or was this meant to not be taken seriously?

Racial discrimination issues involving blacks can be the most exasperating thing a manager has to deal with. The frustration comes from the following sources:

A. Let's be blunt. White discrimination against blacks still exists. Certainly, it is only practiced by a small minority of generally unsophisticated people. Unlike the days before the civil rights movement, discrimination is now usually accomplished with more stealth and generally hidden under numerous guises. Even so, it does happen. For a mature manager, especially a *white* mature manager, to tell me that racism and discrimination don't exist qualifies as one of two things: either the person is a liar, or else they are a sandwich short of a picnic.

B. Some black persons refuse or resist full assimilation into American society. I know that many people will strongly disagree with me. Yes, as individuals, blacks have made dramatic advances in all areas of society, including politics. Our diversity as a nation is also our strength. However, diversity means an assortment, a mixture. It doesn't mean *division*. When a self-recognized group of people decides that they will form teams or organizations which exclude other people not recognized by the group, it only serves to divide even further. How would any race or minority feel if they saw these organizations on television and in print: Caucasian Wine Tasting Society, White Airline Pilots Assn, Miss White USA Pageant, National Society for White Engineers, Caucasian College Fund, and White Entertainment Television (WET?) Do you hear the weeping and gnashing of teeth? I have found more than eighty national organizations that cater to blacks. All or at least most of them are well-meaning organizations founded by people who thought they were doing the right thing. However, these racially-oriented associations only drive in wedges and, frankly, contribute to the aforementioned discrimination by whites. At one time, we desperately needed some of these institutions. Now, I think we have moved far beyond that point.

C.   The youth-inspired so-called *black culture* continues to grow. Young, urban blacks have kidnapped black culture and turned it into a negative. Achieving good grades in school is bad. The blacks' own frequent use of the "N" word in everyday conversation is confusing to other ethnic groups. This is the group primarily responsible for the continuing trend of out-of-wedlock babies and absentee fathers, or as we say on the ranch, "They ate supper before they said grace." In time, we learn to view the culture of violence and crack cocaine as a way of life rather than an aberration. Today's hip-hop and gangsta rap, which contains bigoted, filthy, violence-glorifying language, makes complaints against white, Asian, or Hispanic use of bigoted language appear extremely hypocritical. Career advancement is *acting white*. Listen to the black lyrics booming from open windows, demeaning women and lionizing the thug life. Unless we reverse this trend, racism, and consequently black discrimination, will continue to

164

exist. The self-appointed Jesse Jackson and Al Sharpton, representing the once-proud civil rights movement, continue to divide our nation by portraying blacks as victims. When a white celebrity does something stupid and sticks his foot in his mouth, Jackson and Sharpton loudly trumpet these isolated, rare events as proof that racism is prevalent in our society. Unlike Reverend Martin Luther King, Jr., they divide rather than unite. It reminds me of the way union bosses and labor relations departments keep each other artificially upset. It lines their pockets and keeps them from getting honest work. Unfortunately, I don't believe that the majority of blacks want to be represented by the current so-called leadership. Conversely, I believe most whites think that Sharpton and his ilk accurately represent the views of black America.

Whether you like it or not, white discrimination against blacks exists for three reasons: 1) Some whites believe blacks are lazy—both physically and intellectually. 2) Some whites believe blacks will be looking for ways to sue them for discrimination once they are hired. 3) Some whites believe blacks are more prone to commit criminal acts. It is going to take a lot of work on both sides to reverse this perception. I don't have the answers. However, we can't start repairing the barn roof until we identify the leaks. Find the rot, fix the problem.

D. Let's use some candor and talk about another black issue that has become a problem and will continue to grow: the now commonplace practice of naming black children strange names. Supposedly, this practice is to accentuate African culture. I had not considered this a harmful practice until I read *Freakonomics* by Levitt and Dubner. In their insightful book, the authors point out the societal damage done by this practice of naming our children odd, unusual, unpronounceable names. Once again, this is division, not assimilation and *E pluribus unum.* The people who give their children distinctively black names are usually unmarried, low-income, undereducated mothers. They have low expectations for themselves and obviously for their children. Will a company invest time, money and energy interviewing people named DeAndre and Deja? Alternatively, might they instead prefer to interview Jacob and Molly? Is the company official a racist for not calling DeAndre and Deja in for an interview? Maybe companies do have racism in their deepest cores. Certainly segments of black society do still have major issues that tend to raise red flags in the hiring process. The plight of black urban communities still exists. Poor parenting is evident. Disproportionate numbers of missing fathers are still the norm. Educational leaders continually fail to educate our black youth. Could a face-to-face interview overcome these hurdles? We may never know. Often, we never interview these people. The company official may believe that people named DeAndre and Deja are from disadvantaged backgrounds, knowing that these people tend to turn over quickly, have high absenteeism, and are more likely to claim discrimination charges whenever discipline occurs. If you want to name your child Ebony, go right ahead. It's a free country. Just remember the disadvantage you are placing on this innocent child.

Assimilation should be our goal. As our nation faces challenges with education, manufacturing, health care, and radical Islamist terrorists wanting to kill us, a wise person would think that we would want to unite toward common goals and return to the top ten lists. Instead, we are heading in the opposite direction. We are dividing our nation with Indian reservations, strange-sounding names, racial organizations, Mexican flags, and continued discrimination by whites. The division is driven by the discrimination, and the division drives the discrimination. We are in an endless loop. To correct this, leaders must face this loop and find a way to escape it.

On the bright side, look at how many people are trying to get into the United States versus the number trying to get out. We must be doing something right.

Back in the early '60s, my dad invited a coworker to church. The coworker was a middle-aged black woman. After feeding the cattle and chickens on Sunday morning, we headed off to the little white church and took our usual place near the front pews. The church service was in full swing when the black woman entered the front door. The service stopped as everyone twisted in his or her seat to get a better look at the late arriver. As she started to walk down the aisle in search of an empty seat, one of the elders stood up and raised his hand like a traffic cop. He said, "You'll need to sit on the back row." My father rose from his seat and said, "She can sit with us."

I have always been proud to be called a rancher.

(Answer to the first chapter quiz: Sir Edmund Hillary and Tenzing Norgay were the first climbers to reach the summit of Mount Everest. How many forgot about the little brown Nepalese Sherpa? A Google search of Edmund Hillary resulted in 1,040,000 hits. Tenzing Norgay got a paltry 18,900. According to these numbers, the white European gets a resounding ninety-eight percent of the attention, while the brown person from Nepal gets a paltry two percent.)

Lesson from the Ranch

A good horse never comes in a bad color.

27

Run (When to)

"Leave your simple ways behind, and begin to live;
learn to use good judgment."
Proverbs 9:6

"When your horse dies, get off."
Cowboy Wisdom

In addition to being self-employed in consulting and ranching, over a period of thirty-eight years I have worked for seven national and international companies. I worked at one place for ten years and another for twenty-two years (and praise be, still counting). The other five places failed to live up to my expectations, so I left in short order. Life is far too short to waste time and energy working for a place you don't like. This is not to say that I advocate leaving a job without having a place to go. Only losers and deadbeats do this. However, there are always conspicuous signs pointing to a different career or employer path. Listen to your gut instincts. Then make a plan to change jobs and stick to it. The following indicators warn when it is time to pack up your office. Some are so obvious as to border on ridiculous, but I point them out anyway because I have seen so many managers fail to heed the warnings and suffer the consequences. Every path in life has a few puddles. Life is about straddling the mudholes and enjoying the walk. Therefore, in no particular order, here we go.

Repeatedly, we tell some people that if things don't improve, *termination is pending*. How obvious is this? But then again, I have seen numerous people disregard these warnings. Their incompetent boss prolonged the inevitable, creating intolerable suffering before they struck the deathblow. When you are told this, recognize the warning sign and update your résumé. If I want to see torture, I will watch Jack Bauer on *24*.

The company you work for operates on *fear and intimidation*. This management tactic works well in the short term, but it is a recipe for eventual disaster. Fear and intimidation fail to work on me. The only person I fear sleeps soundly by my side every night. However, the concern is not for you; it is for the other ninety-nine point nine percent of the employees who have to keep working there in a gut-wrenching state. I once worked for a company that operated by fear. As I told them as I went out the door, "I fear I am going to have to leave." If the company is not willing to change their style, you should be out buying an up-to-date red tie.

The company *continually loses money*. The key word is continually. We are all going to have up and downs while we chase long-term growth and profitability. However, if they persistently have red ink, unless it is a small vanity company owned by a billionaire, I would be making regular visits to monster.com. If you are hanging around so *everyone can pull together and turn this thing around*, you are probably a little front-loaded with self-importance, or maybe simply foolish enough to think that by staying, you are going to pull this company out of the ditch it dug for itself. You need to get going while the getting is good.

The *stress is too high*. This is not to say the employer has done anything wrong or that you have chosen the wrong career path. Sometimes, it simply means the planets have aligned against you, and things have risen to the boiling point. I am not talking about the normal day-to-day stresses we all have. As long as we continue to live and work, there will be stress. No, the stress I refer to is the kind that puts you at risk for health problems, causes conflict at home, allows your mind to deteriorate, and drives apart the decisions you make from your core beliefs. Often, a good, long vacation will fix this problem. When it doesn't, your health—mental, physical, and spiritual—is far too important to jeopardize for something as simple as a job. Take a long look at yourself and decide what you need to do. Maybe a transfer or a move to a different company is the answer. I can tell you from experience that I have been there, and I have suffered the consequences. My cardiologist and therapist can provide the details.

There is no *fun at work*. The cause doesn't matter. It makes no difference whether it is your fault, their fault, or nobody's fault. Maybe your coworkers left, and you find yourself in a vacuum. Whatever, when work ceases to be fun, it is time to skedaddle. I don't take leaving a company lightly. Therefore, before you rush out into the wild blue yonder, you should strongly consider how you could make the job fun again. If it is beyond your control, spread your wings and look for a fun place to light.

You *hate your boss*. Okay, if that is the way you feel. Nevertheless, I would ask a person who was leaving a job if he had hated *every* boss in his life. I often find this during the interview process. If you dig deep, you will find people out there who have left job after job because they could not get along with their bosses. Oh, they may say their bosses were unfair, or discriminated against them. I have heard how their bosses did not understand their problems or wouldn't honor their requests for time off ... and so forth and so on. Regardless of how it is phrased, it all boils down to hatred for every boss the person has ever had. So who is the real problem here? These people go through life carrying a big grudge. As the cowboys say, "It doesn't take a very big person to carry a grudge."

You are *bored* out of your mind. Many people would happily change places with someone who was bored on the job. (See the above paragraph on stress.) However, if you don't find the job challenging and find the tasks at hand tedious, it would be a good time to look for an office with a different view. Of course, you could ask your supervisor to find challenging, rewarding things for you to do. You might even seek out opportunities within the company. If your boss has even a minuscule of leadership in his bloodstream, he will help you in your search. Who knows? You may not need to leave after all.

Your employer has *poor ethics*. The company requests you do something that is illegal, immoral, or just simply makes you queasy. Maybe you are not directly involved, but breaches of ethics happen around you all the time. If you are not in a position to put a stop to this mess, then you have to turn in the badge. I would do this with the utmost speed before you go to jail with the rest of them.

Your *values* differ from the company's. Different companies operate on different value systems. Most of the time, you can make minor adjustments to your personal value system in order to have inner peace, or depending on your level of influence, you may even convince the company to make minor adjustments to theirs. If neither is possible, then you need to buy the best suit you can afford and line up your interviews. Whatever you make will not be worth the price you will pay if you stay. What is a ton of misery worth nowadays?

You used to be *in the loop*, but now you are not. The boss no longer laughs and jokes with you. Your coworkers are still smiling and pleasant, but you sense a distance between you. People stop talking when you enter a room. Meetings transpire, and you are not invited. Your phone doesn't ring as often, and the only emails you get are spam. I have known a few people who had these perceived experiences, and they were simply paranoid. They needed medication, not a new job. However, remember that you are not paranoid if it is true. If these things are happening to you, move fast and counterattack. The hourglass is down to a few stubborn grains. You should be networking as fast as possible to find a new company.

As a source of personal irritation, I sure get tired of interviewing people, usually managers, who tell me the reason they are leaving their current employer is lack of opportunities or lack of advancement potential. This is funny when a majority of them are coming to me from Fortune 500 companies, or even Fortune 50 companies. Let's see, their present employer has locations in twenty states, their sales were $7 billion last year, and they have more than one hundred thousand employees. Yet they don't have the opportunity to advance? Please quit peeing on my back and telling me it is rain. Honesty is still a virtue.

What kind of lessons from the ranch can we learn from all of this? I think it is the cowboy philosophy of knowing who you really are, refusing to be flexible in your values, and finding that once you get your mind straight, life can be a whole lot of fun. Know when to run and when to stay. Don't destroy yourself trying to make a dollar for somebody else.

Lesson from the Ranch

A bumblebee is considerably faster than a John Deere. Know when to park and run for cover.

CHAPTER

28

Safety

"If you want to live securely in the land,
follow my decrees and obey my regulations."
Leviticus 25:18

"Don't squat with your spurs on."
Cowboy Wisdom

attle are dangerous beasts. Greenhorns usually underes timate the power that cattle have. Our nation's grave yards are full of people who got close and personal with a raging bull or found themselves at the bottom of a stampede. A cow can weigh one thousand pounds or more; while bulls can run over two thousand pounds. A cold, hard fact is that cattle can kill you anytime they chose. No one can ever know what is going through an animal's mind at any given moment. Ranchers quickly learn about flight zones and animal behavior. We design handling corrals, chutes, and pens with safety in mind—for the cowboy and for the cattle. As you work the cattle, a stray shadow, a barking dog, a car horn, anything unusual can frighten the animals and set them off. If you are in the way, you are going to lose that sumo match. In addition, the ranch kills many cowboys when their horses throw them.

Whether your employees work in a service environment or a manufacturing setting, safety should be one of your three top concerns. When Henry Ford was asked what he considered the most important item with regards to production, quality, and safety, he responded with his own question, "What's the most important leg on a three-legged stool?"

Safety— and the lack thereof—has a monetary cost. When you speak to top management about safety, it is a good rule to talk in dollars and cents. They really understand that language. They will politely nod in agreement when you talk about the other aspects of safety, but money is their comfort zone and you will get quick buy-in. Over and above the workers' compensation expense, hidden costs such as lost productivity and training time, emotional impact on witnesses, and company image will at least triple the reported medical expenses. Don't forget to calculate these costs.

Safety has traditionally been a part of human resources management, but lately the trend has been to separate safety into its own department. I disagree with this approach. I believe safety is a people issue, and thus should be a part of an organized, systematic human resources department. It is people who commit unsafe acts, and people who allow unsafe conditions to exist.

Unfortunately, most safety actions are reactive rather than proactive: someone probably has to get hurt before a problem is fixed. We may throw tools, procedures, guards, disciplinary action, college degrees, and even the kitchen sink at trying to be proactive, but the real fix comes after someone is hurt. This isn't to say that safety in the workplace in general isn't improving. Over the decades, safety has improved impressively. Even so, we have a long way to go in protecting our sons and daughters from danger.

Whether I am working at my management job, consulting with other companies, or working on the ranch, I strive for the best solutions for creating a safe environment, using tried and true methods that work everywhere they are applied. There are four categories I always refer to when trying to make a task or environment safe. One of the four will always work.

1. **Radical Solution**. What is the goal of the job? Is there an entirely different way to accomplish the goal? Many ranchers have stopped using small, square, hand-handled bales of hay and switched over to the eight hundred-plus round hay bales, which are handled with a tractor. It has eliminated back, shoulder, and arm injuries. Another example is the way we drive in steel T-posts when building a barbed wire fence. We used to drive these into the ground with a hand-held driver. The driver was awkward, and depending on the firmness of the ground, it could take up to twenty licks to get a T-post in the ground. Then someone came up with the idea that the hydraulic bucket on the tractor could drive the T-posts. With a little downward stroke of the bucket, the T-post now sinks into the ground without a grunt; once again removing another potential cause of human injury. Look at the goal of the task, and use your creativity to develop radical solutions.

2. **Reduced Frequency Solutions**. How can you decrease the number of times a job has to be done? When building fences, we would travel to town (vehicle accidents), purchase the supplies needed for the job, and then unload the items at

the ranch (muscle/bone injuries). We finally got smart and started ordering fencing supplies in bulk,. making it the vendor's responsibility to bring the supplies to the ranch and unload in the barn. Not only did this solution reduce our risk of injury, but it also saved considerable time and money.

3. **Environment Solutions**. What aspect of the environment can I change to eliminate or reduce the hazard? A friend recently installed a roof over his cattle-working chute, with lights under the roof. This way, he can work his cattle at night, avoiding the summer heat; which in turn keeps him and his cowboys from getting heat exhaustion or from having to work too quickly and unsafely to beat the dimming light. As a bonus, because stress in cattle reduces the grade of beef, working the cattle at night and keeping them from baking in the summer sun also improves the overall quality of beef. Once again, the safer method also equals dollar savings.

4. **Procedure Solution.** When all else fails, use a procedure solution. To me, this is the weakest of the four, because it relies solely on the human element. In other words, we must depend on the person doing the job to adhere to the new procedure. Procedural solutions take time to develop and implement and are hard to enforce. In addition, we often find that the procedure is inadequate, or that the process changed without a corresponding change in the procedure. Nevertheless, when managed properly, a procedural solution can prevent accidents and save lives. The simplest procedures are the best and are usually no-brainers. I used to call the cattle to the barn and then feed them grain. Trying to put the grain into the feed troughs was hazardous, as the cattle,

in their excitement, would bump me around and step on my feet. They didn't mean to hurt me; like me, they are just not very bright. Now, I place the grain in the feed troughs and then call them to eat. Very simple, and it reduces my chance of injury.

The main purpose of this chapter is to convince you that accidents are preventable. A great manager will demand a safe work environment for his or her employees, regardless of the reporting structure. For me, it is not about the money. Never has been, and never will be. Of course, when I talk to management about safety, I always talk in terms of expense, but that is simply a means to an end. It is really about sending the father home with all digits intact; or that carpal tunnel syndrome doesn't torment the children's mother. My moment of clarity comes when I place my own children in the shoes of my employees. That makes my purpose clear.

Lesson from the Ranch

The safer the trail, the faster the cattle get to Kansas.

29

Self-Importance

"Let someone else praise you, not your own mouth —
a stranger, not your own lips."
Proverbs 27:2

"He thinks the sun came up just to hear him crow."
Cowboy Wisdom

Years ago, I had a neighbor who lived down the road. He wore expensive cowboy boots and a big Stetson hat. More times than not, you would see him riding his horse on his ranch or sometimes down the road. He was "as full of wind as a corn-eatin' horse," which is just a country way of saying he was rather prone to boasting. According to him, he was the only real rancher in those parts. He was the only one who knew how to raise cattle, and he was quick to tell you how stupid you were. He was full of self-importance. Inadvertently running into him would spoil your whole day. As time went by, it turned out that he was not a big operator but maintained a very small herd of low-quality cattle. , He was also an alcoholic, who made his real living bootlegging whiskey. He was riding his horse because he had lost his driving license. When he passed away, he left very little to his family. Rather than the picture of a proud, successful man, he had turned out to be a pathetic person. His existence on this Earth had affected everyone he met.

We all have worked with a self-important person. I included this character in the book because of the negative impact such people can have at the workplace. It is my belief that human resources should be the one to deal with these obnoxious people, because HR has the skills. Most other departments don't.

So how do we define self-important people? Well, for starters, they are arrogant and have a half-baked opinion on every issueThey can be very critical and judgmental of their coworkers. These pompous buffoons want everyone to view them as special. To fit their self-designated status, they strut around the workplace and spout words of perceived wisdom. All of their energy focuses on the mirror, and they usually never hear a word you say, unless of course you speak their name. They make loud proclamations on a variety of subjects that are not only wrong but also dangerous to the unaware. When they are wrong, they get defensive. Self-important people constantly maintain a wall between themselves and others., I may be wrong, but I have never seen such a person relaxed. I am not even sure they sleep. They are always ready to impart their obnoxious personas onto anyone within hearing distance. Their departments or areas are far more important than anyone else's, and the rules don't apply to them. They avoid taking responsibility for anything; they are too important for blame. Usually, they are male. In all my years, I have encountered only a few females I would identify as self-important. This may just be a highly skewed observation, but I really think self-importance is a predominately male trait, perhaps left over from our days on the savannah when every tribe had competing alpha males. Too bad we are still not in the Cro-Magnon days. We could just hit them over the head with a stick and be done with it.

Do you know people like this? If so, they need to be controlled. They hurt your organization in these ways:

1. They stifle creativity by attacking ideas not their own.

2. They devastate morale due to stress.

3. They lower productivity.

4. They drive away competent employees.

I am not a psychiatrist or psychologist and could not begin to dissect these creatures. With that said, I have observed through the years patterns that are helpful in discovering why such people feel the need to project arrogance. To determine how to deal with them, it is important to know *why* they are the way they are.

To begin, I believe self-important people generally feel inferior and suffer from a bad case of insecurity. This causes them to become extremely self-conscious; never able to relax and let their true (good) side show. Instead, they cover up this insecurity with all of the above behaviors, driving everyone else insane. In addition, I find most self-important, pompous people are really—deep down—jealous of others' abilities, skills and intelligence. Maybe when they were kids, the team picked them last. Perhaps an older sibling may have been their parents' favorite child, who knows? and who really cares? Every single day everyone is fighting their own personal and professional battles. Who has time to delve into someone else's private demons? What we do care about is how to deal with these egocentric sociopaths.

183

Let us apply the ranch approach to this problem. People are seldom honest with self-important people. They will either tend to avoid, or else go along with the self-important behavior: but both choices will result in gastrointestinal distress. Therefore, the best approach is straight on; but privacy is crucial. Trying to correct their behavior in public will only pour gas on the fire. With self-important people, it helps to remember that they are actually fragile and must be handled with care — that is, assuming you do want to salvage them and turn them into a productive team member. If you don't want to fix the problem and simply want them to disappear, just start challenging them in public, such as in the conference room. They will soon blow a gasket.

But if you do want to salvage them, the next time you notice them being critical of others or suffocating someone else's creativity, pull them into a private area. Once you are alone, start by praising them. I know it is hard, but try to come up with something positive to say. Then be brutally honest and tell them that their behavior is having a negative effect on the workforce. Be specific about what the effect is and how it harms the bottom line. Don't ease into it or chew around the edges, but face it straight on. Like most bullies, self-important people cannot handle a straight punch to the nose. It makes their eyes water, ears ring, and pretty much disorients them for a while. Nevertheless, as with the bully, this does start their journey of reviewing their own behavior and its consequences. The next day, remind them of their place on the team. Remind them of how important they are. Now would be a good time to praise them again. You may have to hold your nose, but this is part of the job. If you can't do it, they say running a live bait shop is relatively stress-free. Like shampoo, you may have to rinse and repeat a couple of times. If their behavior changes, you win. If they leave the company, you win. If nothing changes, you haven't lost anything; and you sleep better knowing you tried. Therefore, the odds are three out of three that you win. What's holding you back?

The following is a true story validated by several associates. Back on 9/11 when terrorists attacked the World Trade Center towers, a VP requested an emergency meeting. He asked all managers to attend and to bring their staff. Everyone gathered in the conference room, which was standing room only. Understand that most of the people were in shock over the events that had happened that day and desperately needed reassurance that the world was not ending. The VP entered the somber room and asked for everyone's attention. He then announced that he had asked his girlfriend to marry him, and she had said yes. Wedding plans were tentative, and he would let everyone know the date once it was solidified. He wanted everyone to know so there wouldn't be any rumors about him floating around. After a long, uncomfortable pause, someone, in a low voice, expressed congratulations. With that, he dismissed the meeting. He never mentioned that morning's events of terror.

Lesson from the Ranch

Sometimes, the village idiot and the self-important person are one and the same.

185

Sexual Harassment

"Can a man scoop a flame into his lap and
not have his clothes catch on fire?
Proverb 6:27

"Always drink upstream from the herd."
Cowboy Wisdom

Seldom do you ever hear the words sexual harassment and cattle ranching in the same sentence. Most would assume that ranching and farming are male-dominated activities, and thus that opportunities for harassment are nil to none. However, this is not true. At auctions, equipment dealers, rodeos, there are plenty of women to harass. Women own some farms and ranches; in fact, it is common. Two hundred thirty-seven thousand women are the primary owner/ operator on farms and ranches nationwide: over eleven percent of the total. Of the 2.1 million U.S. farms, 852,000 of which raise cattle, why do we not hear anything about sexual harassment? Is there a lesson here?

Eliminating sexual harassment in the workplace is very simple. First, you develop a policy of zero tolerance. Second, you train your management team until you are blue in the face. Third, as the cowboys say, "Never draw unless you're really going to shoot." If you suspect a quid pro quo situation or if a hostile environment is brewing, take a firm stand and put an immediate halt to it. Would termination solve your problem? If so, roll up your sleeves and do it. Instead of termination, some companies may want to move a potential harasser around in the organization, but moving a bad apple is like moving cancer around your body. It may hurt less in the brain than the lung, but who is fooling who? This is asking for disaster. To maintain a place of employment with high ethics, you must jettison the bad apples. I see sexual harassment as a severe violation, so I don't give second chances. I used to, but found I was only fooling myself. Without surgical intervention, you are not going to turn that bull into a steer.

You should be wary, however, of false accusations. Sometimes, employees frame supervisors for sexual harass-ment as a way of getting back at them. I have seen this occur so many times that I have begun to think of it as the norm. After receiving disciplinary action, an employee—often with the help of others—will concoct a sexual harassment tale involving the supervisor. The poor jerk never knew what hit him, and he finds himself on the unemployment line. The way to guard against these attacks is to keep your behavior beyond reproach. If a supervisor has a reputation of flirting or using innuendos, he will find his defense weak when he is falsely accused of sexual harassment. A professional manner will enable a supervisor to weather most accusation storms.

Another area of caution is to be aware of harassment even when it goes unreported. Many studies have found that most women don't report harassment even after it reached intolerable proportions, preferring to resign their position rather than go through the horrors of a sexual harassment investigation. This is where the competent manager comes into play. We should not be sitting behind our desks and waiting for a situation to reach the status of a *formal* complaint. We must be proactive, and as Barney Fife said, "Nip it in the bud." Many people don't want to take a proactive approach because doing so may alienate or upset an associate. However, to choose not to do anything when you know that harassment is occurring is a good sign that you have chosen the wrong profession. We should never be afraid of upsetting the apple cart. Even if the harasser is in a higher-level position than you are, to sit back and just watch it happen borders on criminal. If you don't have enough authority, your new job is to find someone who does.

One thousand and one activities can be considered as fostering a hostile work environment. Quid pro quo hides its ugly face under many masks. Our jobs are to expose this blight in whatever form it takes. Your company will be more profitable in terms of the bottom line, while reducing your legal exposure. Competent, professional people will prefer to work for your company. Especially, formerly sexually harassed people will now be free from this terrible fear.

Lesson from the Ranch

A man that can't control his actions is no man at all.

CHAPTER 31

Spiritually Connected

"And what do you benefit if you gain the whole world but are yourself lost or destroyed?"
Luke 9:25

"Always travel with your pistol, jerky and Bible. These three things can getcha out of any tight spot."
Cowboy Wisdom

Spirituality

Years ago I discovered that our struggles in management must be guided something bigger than ourselves. How I made this personal discovery would require another book. Suffice it to say that it is a firm belief of mine. To separate your spiritual life from your professional life will certainly weaken and perhaps destroy both. To this end, as you will have noted, each chapter in this book starts with an applicable verse from the Bible and sometimes also contains spiritual lessons to assist you in your profession. While this book is certainly not a religious tome, an atheist or agnostic might be upset by this theme. If you fall into these categories, it is my sincere hope that you will read on anyway. Now would be a good time to make the point that I have no qualms with Jews, Muslims, Buddhists or those who practice the Hindu religion. In fact, I encourage all spirituality anywhere I find it. I do not ascribe to the "I'm right, you're wrong" school of thought. Most people practice the religious beliefs of their parents or geographical region. Had I been born and raised in Syria, I would be a Muslim. If I had started out in Tibet, I would be a Buddhist. However, I did not; I was born and raised by Christian parents in a region of the world where the majority is Protestant. No mystery here. It is a simple matter of the draw. All of the religious conflicts throughout history and even in the modern day have been about whose religion was right. Today's so-called War on Terror is not about terrorism, but rather a religious war being fought between Islam and Christianity with the Jews thrown into the mix. I hope that someday everyone will mature and stop the 'my God is bigger than your God' playground scene. It will not happen in our lifetime or our children's or grandchildren's but I can dream. Okay, I will stop this babbling regression and get back to the topic.

As a young American nation moved westward, white Christian Protestants established most of the new settlements. Therefore, these values and beliefs are engrained in the rural, western lifestyle. As a result, ranches and farms are, more often than not, spiritually based. That doesn't mean that farmers and ranchers are especially devout people. Sometimes, they are loud, cussing, hard-drinking, fist-fighting, ring-tailed tooters. However, in the calm of the day and the quiet of night, they do believe in a higher power. They realize that everyone has a divine spark and, for the most part, live their lives accordingly.

The ranch also tends to weed out weak personalities, people who think that they could get by simply by harassing someone weaker than them. There is too much hard work, too many lean times. To survive the long haul takes deep resolve and maturity. Ranch people live by the western creed that a cowboy must never shoot first, never hit a smaller man, never take unfair advantage. Inner strength and maturity are not ingredients in the recipe for failure .

Spirituality is the way you find maturity and inner strength in your life. Understand that spirituality and organized religion are only somewhat connected. Religion can play an important role in your spiritual health. However, one of the most spiritual men I ever knew (his name was Tolbert) never set foot inside a church. Even so, he lived and died in a way that would make most preachers hang their heads in shame.

To start with, you need to know who you are. Not who you used to be or who you plan to become. Who are you right now? What are your values? How do you perceive yourself? How do others think of you? Are you happy with yourself, or do you wish every morning you were someone else? Until you can answer these questions and others like them, repairing your spiritual health will be difficult.

Once you know who you are, you need to realize that you connect to everything in the universe. This sounds a little mystical. Well, we will explore this more deeply in another part of this chapter. Suffice it to say at this point that no man is an island, and his thoughts, actions, and behaviors act on every- one around him. To maintain your spiritual health, you have to help others. You could do this in big, showy ways; but by far the best is to try to help everyone you contact in a small but meaningful way. Make a positive difference, however small, in your own way. It is almost impossible to feel sorry for yourself when you are helping a struggling employee learn a new task, assisting a neighbor repair his storm damage, or teaching a child how to deal with a bully.

To maintain your spiritual health, you have to commit the time and effort, just as you would with any other important endeavor. Even people who recognize the supreme importance of spirituality still fail to set aside enough time in the day for its maintenance. As the world gets wackier and more out of balance, we should be devoting more time to our spiritual health, not less. These activities may include doing volunteer work or listening to inspirational music; or, better yet, make your own music, paint a picture (who cares if you haven't been formally trained), spend time in the woods, set aside thinking time, attend religious services, or study (not just read) the New Testament, Torah, or Koran.

All of these activities are suggestions that may or may not work for you. You have to choose something that is comfortable for you. However, I guarantee you that the one thing you absolutely must do is to communicate with God every day. Of course, God goes by many names, but for simplicity, I use the Judeo-Christian name. If you don't connect to God and include Him in every aspect of your daily life, you will never achieve the spiritual health you so desperately need. Without the John Deere as an anchor, the tires and motor are useless.

We perform prayer in many ways. Whatever works for you is great. As for me, I don't pray for material things. I don't ask for money or riches. I don't even ask for good physical health or that new tractor at the dealership. I believe the universe knows what I need and doesn't put too much weight on what I want. What I do ask for is wisdom and understanding.

For those readers who are atheist or agnostic, I would ask you to turn to science for guidance in your belief. That's right: I said science. You may have turned your back on a higher power based on the history of organized religion or the revelations of science. One thing you should bear in mind is that while religion has had a bloody history, religion is ultimately only a fabricated, human-driven device. Just like manufactured governments, brutal power can and will run unchecked at times. Don't blame God for the wickedness that men perpetuate. Maybe you don't see how God can be so unjust as to allow all of the suffering in the world, and therefore you denounce God. For my part, I don't see how God and justice have really anything to do with most of the suffering I see. In fact, I challenge the statement that there is great worldwide suffering. Even in depressed parts of the world, people can be happy and live full lives. I know this is not a popular thing to say, but I am not asking for votes. Even concerning natural disasters, it is only a disaster because humankind decided to get in the way. If I choose to live below a dam or levee, I shouldn't curse God when my house washes away. If I live in a flood plain, I don't see the rich deposit of earth after every flood; I only see where my house used to sit. When my Gulf Coast beach house blows away in a hurricane, I shouldn't sign up for Atheist International. I should, instead, be taking an IQ test to see how much help I really need. We shouldn't blame a deity when the natural order works.

Returning to science: if you find spiritual beliefs contrary to science, then spiritual beliefs are easily viewed as measly superstitions and fallacies. This popular view is simply wrong. Science and religion operate under vastly different parameters. In spite all of the majesty and awe that the scientific world inspires, science is not designed to answer the questions that religion asks. Nor should we use religion to fill in the 'God of the gaps.' Religion should embrace science as it improves our ability to explain how God put things together. In contrast, elites of organized religions often hate the efforts to seek a scientific context for the appreciation of spiritual phenomena, seeking instead to control humanity with doctrine and dogma. Science in its intellectual, methodical, peer-reviewed processes can deepen our wonder and amazement at the power of God. Instead of warring factions, the two sides should encourage each other. I recently saw a newspaper headline that read, "Darwin vs. God, Round 2007: Kansas Declares Darwin Winner." This is wrong on many levels. Splashy headlines are one thing; gross irresponsibility is another. I cannot stress it enough. God and science are not at odds. They never have been. Francis S. Collins, the scientist who leads the Human Genome Project, stated it best : "Science is not threatened by God; it is enhanced."

If one wants to glimpse God at work, instead of listening to highly compensated evangelists, you could spend your time wisely studying quantum mechanics, the uncertainty principle, the second law of thermodynamics, the Big Bang theory, and "Spooky Action at a Distance." As Niels Bohr said, ""Those who are not shocked when they first come across quantum theory cannot possibly have understood it." You have read the Acts of the Apostles. Now read the works of Erwin Schrödinger, Werner Heisenberg, Stephen Hawking, Kip S. Thorne, Paul Davies, and other influential contributors to science. For me, the window through which we gaze at God is not stained glass but a microscope.

If brute intellectual power is more your cup of tea, then I suggest you read the writings of C.S. Lewis and St. Augustine. I find it beyond reason to discuss stress and anxiety without emphasizing the spirit within each of us. Turn your worries over to your Creator, then go tell that self-important, know-it-all what you really think about him. I will let famed astronomer Robert Jastrow wrap up this concluding subject with his thoughts regarding the relationship between science and spirit: "It seems as though science will never be able to raise the curtain on the mystery of creation. For the scientist who has lived by his faith and the power of reason, the story ends like a bad dream. He has scaled the mountains of ignorance; he is about to conquer the highest peaks; as he pulls himself over the final rock, he is greeted by a band of theologians who have been sitting there for centuries."

Connected

Although this is a middle chapter in the book, I procrastinated writing this chapter until the rest of the book was completed. My delay was due to several reasons. First, the subject matter of this sub-chapter can and will be considered by some to be somewhat 'flaky' or silly. If you feel this way, please keep reading. I'll take us back to Earth before the chapter ends. Second, I was not sure what I wanted to say or how to say it. Of course, I knew the basic idea, but I struggled with the proper way to bring it forth. In the end, I finally decided that as managerial professionals, we do need exposure to this subject. Knowledge of this realm makes all the difference between good and great.

I have always harbored a belief that everything on this earth has value. When I was a youngster, my parents, aunts, and uncles made fun of me because I threw a fit if anyone stepped on a bug. In the summertime, I rushed ahead of everyone so I could brush the bugs off the steps leading to whatever building we were headed. I ticked off a cousin one year when I set his frog collection free. Mentally, I could not stand for them to be trapped in a barrel. To this day, I have never shot a game animal. When we were created, we were told we would, "… reign over the fish in the sea, the birds in the sky, the livestock, all the wild animals on the earth, and the small animals that scurry along the ground." If I am going to have dominion over something, I prefer it to be on my plate at suppertime, preferably medium rare.

For me, putting animals to use, whether as food, transportation, or clothing, is an honorable thing to do. On the other hand, killing animals for sport is not for me, though I strongly support hunters' rights to pursue their pleasure. While I myself don't hunt, when my property or my safety is at stake, I turn into a killing machine. If a dog is chasing my calf, you can subtract that dog from the world count.

An idea entered my mind back in my childhood, and I have never been able to shake it: we are all connected. The same scoop of stardust molded humankind and the stars and planets. My childhood feelings about not hurting living creatures extended even to plants and inanimate objects. I thought that houseplants might get lonely if they were not able to 'see' each other when people were absent from the house. Therefore, as a kid, I would move all the plants into the same room. Strange little dude. I thought that slamming a car door too hard might hurt the car's feelings. My parents hadn't heard of medication. Seriously, I spent a good part of my life believing that everything—whether biological or not—was alive and conscious, and that my actions affected the object either positively or negatively. The truth is, I still have lingering residue from this 'condition.'

Had I possessed the math skills, I would have considered a career in physics, particularly theoretical physics. I easily knocked down top grades in history, science, and other subjects, but I had to take both shoes off to count to ten. I figured a bare-footed physicist wouldn't go over too well, so I went into an area where my strength resided. In physics, one of my favorite topics is quantum mechanics—the theory used to describe the processes that take place in the micro-world. Don't think for a second that I fully grasp the theory. Indeed, one-third of my library covers the subject, and I still can't grasp all of the concepts. Even so, I love to read and study this field in my unrequited quest for knowledge. In my simple non-technical language, and as quickly as possible, I will attempt to explain from my perspective how physics states that everything is connected.

In quantum physics, I may have found a partial (and I do mean partial) answer to the long-ago childhood feelings I had about everything being one and the same. In quantum physics, you cannot separate the observer and the observed. The whole is more fundamental than the parts. The universe interconnects in much subtler ways than the mind can grasp. We have found that atoms are just 'ghosts' and cannot be defined without an observer. Even then, our definition is only partial, as we cannot determine both position and velocity. In fact, an atom sometimes acts as a wave and sometimes as a particle, depending entirely on the observer's perspective.

It is not possible to treat widely separated systems as independent. This scientific discovery, known as non-locality, means that everything is connected. Like a two-person sack race at a picnic every particle in the universe has one leg tied in the same sack . Even time and space (space-time) may be composed of the same essence as matter and energy. When I was young, I liked to eat animal crackers. (Okay—I still do.) Some were shaped like elephants and some like giraffes. Each cracker was a very different animal. However, all the crackers were made from the same cookie dough. At their essence, all the animals in the box were the same.

In addition, all matter and events interact with each other not only in space but also in the past, present, and future. Our narrow perception of reality creates an illusion that everything is separate when in fact it is not. Our puny minds are not capable of seeing that the 'elephant cracker' and the 'giraffe cracker' are the same. Our senses don't 'vibrate' at that high a level. It is akin to the blind man feeling the elephant's leg and thinking he is touching a tree trunk. It was a good guess on his part, but only because he could not see the entire beast.

For me, the strangest thing to come out of quantum physics is the EPR paradox, short for Einstein, Podolsky, and Rosen, who together developed the thought experiment in a 1935 paper. They were trying to prove that quantum mechanics is not a complete physical theory; but what they did discover invalidated their original purpose. Simply stated, measurement performed on one part of a quantum system can have an instantaneous effect on the result of a measurement performed on another part. Take, for example, a pair of entangled protons whose quantum spin cancels out. (I am not capable of explaining how in the world you get particles to entangle, even though an experimental physicist does it all the time. Maybe they have *Particle Entanglement for Dummies* in your local bookstore.) Now separate them (one inch or one light-year) and measure the spin of one proton. Because they were paired, measuring the spin of one proton determines the spin of the other. A measurement in one place can have an instantaneous effect on something that may be light years away. For an analogy, go back to the aforementioned picnic sack race. Now imagine that one teammate is in New York and is mugged and shoved to the sidewalk. At the same time the other teammate, living in Shreveport, will also fall to the pavement. This sounds impossible and in the realm of science fiction, but in the subatomic world, this is the everyday reality. Scientists used to think that measurement would tell what the absolute reality was before we measured; but it is only after the proton is measured that the spin is determined. In other words, the two entangled protons are not separate entities until they are measured. The "spooky action at a distance" baffled even Einstein. However, numerous experiments repeatedly validate the 'spooky action.'

If you are a little upset by all of this, remember that famed physicist Niels Bohr stated, "Anyone who is not shocked by quantum theory does not understand it."

We are part of everything in this universe, and that includes your coworkers, bosses, subordinates, and the man who fills up the vending machines. Entangled is our natural state, even before the event that pulled the trigger firing the Big Bang. We remain so to this day. Everything is made of atoms. We know that atoms are both wave and particle, and that once connected, they affect one another forever no matter where they are. Atoms are 99.999999999999% empty space. There is not much "stuff" there to stump your toe on. Atoms are mainly an empty vacuum with particles/waves at the center. A clump of matter doesn't pass through other matter because it is levitating on an electrostatic field. As you hold this book, you are not touching it. The electron cloud around the atoms of this book supplies a charge, which pushes back at the world.

Scientifically, atoms are just parcels of compressed energy, patterned according to mathematical formulae. Change the formula, and you get a cat. Mix the formula a different way, and you get an oak tree. Previously, I used the analogy of animal crackers. Another way to understand is to view our Creator as the Master Chef. The Master Chef can take beef, spices, corn, lettuce, and tomatoes and make a wonderful porterhouse steak dinner with corn and a side salad. Alternatively, he can take the very same recipe ingredients (parcels of energy), grind the meat into hamburger meat, form the corn into masa, chop the lettuce and tomatoes, and create tasty tacos. There is a big difference between a steak dinner and a taco (different price, too); still, both are made from the exact same ingredients—just mixed together in a different way.

We are simply energy that has been converted into matter ($E=mc^2$), and to pure energy we will someday return. In the equation $E=mc^2$, mass and energy are more than equivalent, they are just different forms of the same thing, such as steam and ice. Matter and energy are two poles of the same unity. Shamans and Mystics call this Oneness.

In my childhood belief that everything was connected, I certainly was not blazing a new trail. Science is just now catching up to what every creed and faith have known for generations. Here is a sampler.

- Abraham in the Bible defined the God as the Unity underlying the entire natural world.

- Chief Seattle said, "Humankind has not woven the web of life. We are but one thread within it. Whatever we do to the web, we do to ourselves. All things are bound together. All things connect."

- The Oglala Sioux spiritual teacher, Ed McGaa, remarked, "Interdependence is at the center of all things. The separation between nature and us is a mirage. The perception is the result of ignorance."

- The Buddhist scripture Avatamsaka Sutra says: "All is one." Every being in the universe depends on every other thing and every other being for their existence.

- *The Tao of Physics* looks at scientific concepts paired with consciousness in the practice of Buddhism and Hinduism. This book contains chapters on the Unity of All Things, Space-Time, Quark Symmetries, and Interpenetration. The author, physicist Fritjof Capra writes, "The universe is seen as a dynamic web of interrelated events. They all follow from the properties of the other parts and the overall consistency of their mutual interrelations determines the structure of the entire web."

- Kabalistic teachings state, "think well of everyone." Kabbalah refers to the "cycle of reciprocity": what is going out from your mind is always coming back to you.

Physicists, neuroscientists, and religious thinkers have evolved to where a paradigm shift is happening. The universe we now know is connected, unifying matter, energy, and consciousness. Science is a remarkable process and much needed in this world, but science, by its nature, never asks the question of why we are here. Science can only explain how we view.

At this point, you might be asking, "What in the world does this have to do with people? What's all this mumbo jumbo about?" I have said all of that to say this. This matter means a great deal to me.

All of this is about our chosen profession. In the introduction, I wrote that management is a sacred profession. I meant exactly what I said. As the persons who handle or should handle the bulk of the people issues, we need to remind ourselves to be extra-cautious with our emotions, thoughts and words. Just as the rest of the universe, our emotions, thoughts, and words come from our Creator, and we should be forever mindful of cause and effect, action and reaction. As we deal with that most delicate of creations, the human mind, we need to recall that everything is connected. Our forays into others' lives will cause an emotional response, for good or for bad. These emotions will lead to thoughts, which transfer into action. Everything we do is consequential. There is value—good or bad—to everything we utter.

My observation of a connected world reminds me of events that transpired only a few years ago: not a perfect example, but it comes close. I had a job in HR management in a beautiful part of our state. Janita and I had a large home that sat on top of a small mountain with great views from the front and the back. The job was ideal in that I had great autonomy and very few problems. I also had great relationships with the people I worked with. Then—unexpectedly—the company asked me to transfer to a new town with an operation infamous for its union, legal, and managerial issues. Out of more than twenty locations, the company wanted me to relocate to this one particular site. I told them, "No" with a capital N. I appreciated the challenge, but I was so content with my life that I did not want to change. Besides, my two youngest children lived nearby, and I didn't want to leave them. (Okay, class, can anyone spell over-protective?) Over the next few months, a new vice president assumed the helm, and she took up the mantra of asking me to move to the infamous operation. After a few more rounds of arm-wrestling, I reluctantly relented.

What the company did not know was that my mother-in-law lived in the new town. As my wife and her mother had always lived several hours apart, visits had been infrequent. With our transfer, we would be just down the street. Our moving to this new town would give Janita the chance to visit her mother more regularly.

One day in the first year of our move, Janita was visiting her mother when my wife's youngest brother happened to stop by, whom she had not seen in more than four years. They had a short reunion of sorts with hugs and kisses. If we had not moved to the new town, she wouldn't have had the opportunity to see her brother. Three weeks after the happy reunion, Janita's brother developed a rapidly progressive disorder and unexpectedly passed away. Janita's close presence to her mother during this horrible period made a world of difference for both my wife and mother-in-law. The following year, my mother-in-law became very sick and bedridden. Since we were in the same town, Janita was able to provide care and support for her mother when she needed it the most. Janita was with her mother the night she passed away.

Janita spent the next several months going through her mother's personal belongings. Some of the items were sad and brought tears of sorrow. Other items were happy reminders of past events. These brought tears of joy. She read old letters and cards and, was gradually able to alleviate her grief through this process — a process that had only become available because we happened to have moved to the same town as her mother.

Shortly after this, an opportunity for an internal promotion was presented to me. I applied and was interviewed. During the interview, I was asked if there were any problems with having to relocate and move from my current town. I stated that I had been placed in that town for a reason and that my business there was now complete. I shared some of the brief details with the interviewers. I could tell they felt the same way I did. I got the promotion and relocation. My time in that town was finished. It was time to move on.

The cosmos works in mysterious ways. Sometimes, though, it works in a very straightforward way. The connections are apparent and rather obvious.

Of all the locations available for transfer, I was given that assignment in that specific town. Why not someone else? As I recall, the company had many managers—twenty or more—who were available for transfer. The odds of a transfer alone were astronomical, as the company did very little lateral transferring in the human resources arena. On top of that, I had only a one-in-twenty shot at transferring to that particular town. So I ask, why me? What was special about that specific town? In addition, what was so special about that particular time in history? I suppose a skeptic would chalk it up to coincidence. Very well then. However, a mere coincidence seems to be quite the stretch, given the odds. Years ago I had been given some advice that stated when you hear hoof beats, don't expect to see zebras. To identify this situation as a coincidence would be assigning it to the status of zebras. In other words, look for the obvious before seeking the unusual as an explanation. The reasoning mind sees that there was an obvious intelligent connection between this series of actions and events.

Until some futurist physicist develops a mathematical equation that explains human behavior, all that we have at this point is a glimpse of our connections. We have great power, raw power that is much greater than we can grasp. Like the blind man, we just cannot see the entire beast. Use this great power wisely.

Wisdom

The difference between wisdom and foolishness is that wisdom has its limits. Wisdom is the most important item you can have at the ranch. In fact, if you possess it, wisdom is the most valuable item you take to work with you each day. If you have wisdom in your possession, all other issues fall into place. Rather than write a chapter on wisdom in which I offer examples and suggestions, I will instead use this space to help you understand wisdom and its components.

I am not sure how to define wisdom, but like a high-quality Angus heifer, I know it when I see it. Throughout this book, I have tossed around the word 'wisdom' many times. I keep using this word because wisdom is vital to our ability to be the best managers we can be, particularly when we are dealing with a wide range of people and personalities. The cowboys say that knowledge is knowing the location of every saloon in town. Wisdom is staying out of them. To write about wisdom, I decided I needed to gain more knowledge about wisdom – find the saloons, if you will— so I took the lazy man's route and Googled 'wisdom.' On the very first page of results, I got eighteen different definitions of wisdom. The definitions ranged from the short but incomplete to the long and very ludicrous. My thesaurus provided the words astuteness, acumen, and advisability along with a list of other choices. Obviously, this was not going to help my readers or me. What I needed was a better source. I needed a source that would give me the characteristics of wisdom and break it down into its elements. In addition, this source would need to provide the purpose of wisdom.

I turned to the Bible and started to look for the word 'wisdom' and words or phrases coupled with 'wisdom.' I was mildly surprised and vastly pleased with what I found. The following are the forty Biblical words connected to 'wisdom':

knowledge, discretion, humility, strength, honesty, discipline, joy, sweet, light, insight, spirit, spiritual, beauty, healthy, strong, ability, expertise, intelligence, understanding, riches, gentle, mercy, thanksgiving, salvation, variety, pure, trusted, treasure, honor, glory, blessing, righteousness, sincere, power, better than coral, jasper, gold, crystal, rubies and silver.

The following twelve Biblical phrases are associated with 'wisdom':

Belongs to the aged, balanced and good judgment, not a simple matter, wise counsel, power to do miracles, no favoritism, peace loving, willing to yield, rich in variety, gives you the right words, Christ Jesus is wisdom itself.

These simple words and phrases give us great assistance in defining wisdom. Glancing over these paragraphs, you can get a real feel of wisdom. Still, it takes many adjectives and descriptors to nail wisdom down. Indeed, as the above Biblical phrases tells us, wisdom is not a simple matter.

To achieve wisdom, I believe one would have to be able to attain some (if not all) of the above associated qualities. I used to think that wisdom simply meant intelligence with some common sense thrown in. I used to be wrong. I hope that I am now on the right path. I believe now that if we combine any two or more qualities from the list of wisdom words, we will be on our way to understanding what wisdom is all about. A *strong* person will show *mercy*. A *gentle, spiritual* person will receive *honor* and *glory*. A person who possesses *humility* and *discretion* will obtain *blessings* and *riches*. Try a few combinations yourself. It's fun and the quickest way to gain a fleeting glimpse of this thing we call wisdom.

While I was researching this chapter, I was reminded of all the times the Old Testament described wisdom as female. For some reason, the early scribes placed wisdom in female form. This could simply be ascribing female attributes to an item, the same way we presently do with ships and cars. Then I remembered that the ancient Gnostics gave wisdom the name of Sophia (Óoõíá, Greek for "wisdom"). In fact, some of the apocryphal religious manuscripts named Sophia (Wisdom) as the Holy Spirit of the Trinity. Of course, this esoteric meaning is hidden so well that we can never know its source. Nevertheless, it is still something to reflect upon in connecting wisdom and the female sex. Maybe men need to consider this as they operate in the world through an alpha-male, testosterone stupor. Maybe defeating your enemies may not be as important as persuading them to join your side through kind words and gentle actions. I realize that sometimes we must fight — to do otherwise would be immoral — but we need to anoint the problem with wisdom before we sharpen our swords.

Lesson from the Ranch

The way we conduct ourselves concerning other's lives may very well reverberate for decades to come.

Standing Plans

"Do to others as you would like them to do to you."
Luke 6:31

"Don't interfere with something that ain't botherin' you none."
Cowboy Wisdom

In my younger days, I was a big believer in standing plans: policies, procedures and rules. They focused on organizational circumstances that occur repeatedly. Not that I tended to follow the rules in my personal life, but I felt that they were a strong cohesive force that pulled all employees together toward a corporate goal. A manager much wiser than me taught me how policies, procedures, and rules tie our hands and prevent us from doing the right thing. He taught me to handle each person as an individual and to stop walking around with a policy book under my arm. My mentor and friend died prematurely about a decade ago while sitting at his work desk. I miss his advice and friendship.

Policies (broad guidelines for action), procedures (series of actions), and rules (mandatory actions) have their place in corporate life, but are ultimately valuable only in a very limited sense. Our Congress and our state legislators spend all of their time restricting our freedoms with unnecessary regulations. I believe that every time we enact a law, a freedom is lost. I am not advocating a return to the Wild West, but this has gotten out of hand. The same thing applies to corporations. Often, the accounting and human resources departments, for lack of anything constructive to do, will spend considerable time developing standing plans that are designed to maximize their control and minimize the creative decision making of the people who actually operate the business. The corporate headquarters will disagree with this assessment, countering that standing plans are developed for consistent action across the organization, legal requirements, and channeled thinking: in other words, everyone thinking in the same, specified direction.

There is some truth in both lines of thought. Even so, we should lean toward fewer policies with broader guidelines. Review your policies and see if they are tying your managers' hands. Managers often can't help a truly needy employee due to restrictive policies. Restrictive policies also prevent managers from taking needed action against the people who need to find a new place to work.

Apply procedures only to a limited number of activities. Procedures fit nicely in areas with high turnover . One time, my superiors handed me a corporate procedure to follow for selecting applicants. My instructions were to adhere to the guidelines. The guidelines contained nine actions with twenty sub-steps that, if adhered, to would "provide the X Corporation with the best possible prospect." I threw the guidelines in the trash and never heard another word about them. This was some time back, but I am sure that there is a sycophant sitting at a desk somewhere in that organization gleefully following the interviewing and selecting procedure.

Rules are great in their place, but once again, a manager should have authority to bend, break, or totally disregard a rule, if needed. The situation and circumstances should dictate the action. I fully understand that in the world of wrongful terminations and the resulting legal actions, rules play an important part of the *just cause* notification process. However, many of our existing rules could be lumped under the *reasonable person* clause. Our fear drives our need to invent rules. Our rules prevent creativity and flexibility. Our lack of creativity and flexibility prevent innovation. Our lack of innovation will result in our demise.

I believe that everyone has great potential, and that it is our job as managers to find the key to unlock this well-spring. Policies, procedures, and rules will sometimes throw roadblocks in our way. I don't believe that everyone can become a superstar, even with enough time, attention, and training. Some people just don't fit the job. Again, policies, procedures, and rules prevent us from taking the needed action. I believe that favoritism within the organization can lead to trouble. I also know that I play *favorites* every day. As complex humans, we are going to treat some of our employees differently from others. Of course, I am going to allow more leeway with my better performers. People who work hard for me are going to have more freedom and flexibility to do their jobs. People who don't work hard or tend to annoy everyone are going to find they have a smaller margin of error and far less latitude. There is nothing wrong with that. Indeed, in the natural order of things, it ends up building a stronger organization.

I maintain that every person is the absolute owner of his life and should be free to do as he wishes as long as he doesn't hurt others. I try to operate from the maxim that all human interaction should be voluntary. I strongly support an ethic of self-responsibility. Policies, procedures, and rules are the antithesis of these beliefs. I think that the natural order will take care of most of our problems. As water seeks its own level, so do people. The stream, left to its own devices, will find its way to the river. We don't need to dig the stream a ditch and force its direction. I would rather managers spent their time inspiring their people and making money than administering a cluster of artificial controls.

This having been said, I think I will spend the next few days drafting, reviewing, and implementing a policy for a *Ranch Dress Code*. I have noticed my son looks a little too casual at times, especially on Fridays. I must be losing control.

Lesson from the Ranch

Any idiot can develop a rule. The problem comes when a lot of idiots follow it.

CHAPTER

33

Strategic Planning

*"Though good advice lies deep within the heart,
a person with understanding will draw it out."*
Proverbs 20:5

"Those who fail to plan, plan to fail."
Cowboy Wisdom

Strategic planning is the most important work we perform on the ranch. Otherwise, we will lose our direction and fail. Our five-year strategic plan is sound in principle, but we don't have stone-carved details. As with any enterprise, entropy makes us zig when we had planned to zag. However, the plan is stable. Everyone agrees to the importance of strict adherence, and everyone fully supports it. Tactical planning is a weekly or monthly process and dovetails with our strategic plan. Were it not for these two planning processes, we would be raising goats instead of cattle, growing soybeans instead of hay, and asking the banker for an extension each year. The plan is the ranch, and the ranch is the plan. They are entangled.

In the business world, strategic planning is usually a misnomer. Most strategic plans encompass the next few months, with very few indeed including the next five or ten years. This is a little too much far thinking for some of our executives. Maybe I should not blame them, since our corporate business models rely heavily on stockholders and short-term return on investment. Our industry leaders tend to live in the tactical world; and so it surprises them when the business fails after a few years. This is especially true of small business people. A cold, hard look at the failure rate for small businesses would deter most people from opening up Joe's Sandwich Shop.

Through the years, the human resources profession has certainly evolved. They used to be the hiring-and-firing people. Then they became a little more polished and became the still widely used "personnel managers." As the profession progressed and people begin to analyze the role it played, more emphasis was placed on workforce planning, people development, benefit cost analysis, labor, and employee relations. Slowly, the titles changed to reflect the employee as resource to be cultivated; and Human Resources began to look more like a profession than an unavoidable evil.

The missing link in this evolution was the reluctance of top management to value HR's role in strategic planning. The HR professionals were at fault for not seeking a *seat at the table*. As top management slowly wised up and people professionals begin to push, the last few years have seen more and more people involvement in planning, both strategic and tactical. The HR professionals are getting better at learning planning methods that identify assumptions, risks, and environmental factors. Still, in most situations, they are not true strategic partners.

It is my firm belief that managers should spend at least twenty percent of their time in the planning process. In an eight-hour day, we should be spending at least an hour and a half on planning. If the bogged-down manager is too busy in the daily grind of inputting data, writing reports, and putting out fires, he or she needs to rethink his work model and come up with a better plan. Too many times, due to the demands of local and corporate management, managers find themselves in the role of a clerk. How a person divorces himself from the clerical role and becomes a true manager is up to that particular individual within that particular situation.

So how can managers engrain themselves in the strategic planning process? Maybe the following suggestions are a good place to start.

1. Identify the difference between strategic and short term. They are dissimilar beasts, battled with different weapons. Find out what your organization's operational definitions are for the different types of planning. Just because something is important to the organization doesn't mean it is strategic. However, if it is strategic, you can bet their bottom dollar it is important.

2. Know your business inside and out. Who are the customers? What does quality look like? What technologies are important? How can you be a starting tailback when you haven't learned the game?

3. When discussing the business with management, talk in strategic terms. If it walks like a duck and quacks like a duck, it is probably a duck. If you

want upper management to view you in a strategic light, you need to quack in strategic terms.

4. Evaluate people effectiveness in all activities as they relate to the strategic plan. If it's broke, fix it. If it works, enhance it. Our people strategic plans must tie in with the organization's overall plan. Don't bring your knife to a gunfight. Make sure you have a round for every chamber.

5. Play a key role in leadership training and developing a culture that will adhere to the strategic plan and ensure its success. A truthful assessment of reality is a good place to start when evaluating leadership and culture. The mirror is always a good place to start when you want to pull yourself together.

6. Shape the organization's policies so they dovetail with the strategic plan. Often our policies and our plans go off on tangents. Make sure they stay together.

7. Keep informed about state and federal legislative proposals. Your strategy will need to change accordingly. Besides, you will look smart when you start discoursing on the various bill numbers and the legislative strategies.

8. Finally, make sure you design the organization's plans to produce unmistakable results: can they be tracked and quantifiably measured rather than graded by nebulous words and phases? Use your creative talents to develop new ways to measure success.

As previously noted, we operate the ranch with a sound plan. In the early stages, without the plan, we would have failed. I will admit that at times it was hard to stick to the plan. There were things I wanted to do differently, causing me to toss and turn at night. I was frustrated that I couldn't do it better and faster or, as they say, neater, sweeter, and more completer. But instant gratification is never part of a strategic plan. The lesson I learned on the ranch was to put a tremendous amount of thought into the plan, to stick to it no matter what occurred, and finally and most importantly, to end each plan with a prayer. Whether you are at the helm of a Fortune 500 company, operating a sushi bar, or raising cattle, you cannot do it alone.

Lesson from the Ranch

To operate without a plan should be preceeded with planning not to get out of bed. It'll save you time and misery.

CHAPTER
34

Stress

"Don't worry about anything; instead, pray about everything. Tell God what you need, and thank him for all he has done."
Philippians 4:6

"Forgive your enemies. It messes up their heads."
Cowboy Wisdom

In the cattle industry, stress plays a crucial role in your ranch's profitability. When you harvest your beef, too much stress at the ranch and in the transportation process can cause your cattle to be known as dark cutters. Dark cutting beef is darker and drier than good-quality beef. The value of this beef is lower due to its undesirable color, off-flavor taste, and shortened shelf life. In scientific terms, dark cutting beef is due to a high pH value of 5.8 or above.

High pH is caused by an abnormally low concentration of lactic acid. This low concentration is the result of an inadequate content of glycogen in the muscles. Glycogen breakdown is caused by increased amounts of adrenaline released in the body. Adrenaline production invariably increases during stressful situations.

Just as with our lives, stress in cattle can erupt from a variety of sources. Cold, rainy weather can induce stress and result in dark cutters; as can extremely hot weather. Large fluctuations in temperature occurring over short periods can also cause dark cutters. The way we handle cattle during transportation and while at the feed yard can have a major impact on the beef quality. A stressful, crowded holding yard staffed by cowboys who shout, beat the cattle, and behave like buffoons will always increase adrenaline, thereby lowering the beef quality. The fastest and surest way to lower the quality of your beef is to mix strange animals prior to harvesting. Mixing different groups of cattle results in an excited mental state as psychological skirmishes break out to establish a new "pecking order." The worst situation regarding the deterioration of beef quality is when you mix bulls. The mental and physical struggle to be the alpha male can cause dark cutters within ninety minutes. We are not talking about bumps and bruises; we are referring to the chemical change in the meat itself due solely to stress. That is the speed and severity of stress onset. Any rancher worth his salt is well aware—or should be—of these conditions, and realizes that stress costs money.

If stress in a simple-minded animal like a cow can cause profound and rapid deterioration, just imagine what stress can do to a complex human being. Modern medicine has only recently begun to comprehend the impact of stress in our lives. Your doctor realizes that stress is a killer. A noxious work environment will leave you feeling rundown and anxiety-ridden at best. At worst, it can cause so much stress that you become physically sick – and not the mild forms of sick, such as a stomach bug or head cold, but dangerously sick:

- Your passive-aggressive coworker can cause you stress that will give you the gift of high blood pressure, abnormal heartbeat (arrhythmia), blood clotting issues, and atherosclerosis. Stress also triggers coronary artery disease and heart attacks. Your death will only please the coworker and the funeral home. Well, at least you will be going to your grave knowing that someone will be getting pleasure out of your early death.

- People who have jerks for bosses tend to have various muscle pains caused by stress-induced tension. A disgruntled boss can even lead to rheumatoid arthritis. That's okay. Your children will understand that your back spasms prevent you from playing catch. The boss certainly trumps the kids. Am I correct? After all, when did the kids ever give you a paycheck?

- The self-important, know-it-all down the hallway can deliver stress to your cubicle that can bring about gastroesophageal reflux disease, peptic ulcer disease, and irritable bowel syndrome. You always thought he made you sick. Now you know.

- An overloaded work schedule can result in painful menstrual periods, decreased fertility, and erection problems. The $40 a week that you make in forced overtime is worth every penny of your non-functional reproductive system. Besides, who has time for a love life? Your life is rich enough. With any luck, you'll receive the three percent annual increase.

- A mind-numbing, repetitive, meaningless job with no chance for advancement will generate stress that can worsen your asthma and chronic obstructive pulmonary disease. Oh well, your job is certainly worth a portion of your oxygen. Blue lips are not that bad. They have been selling lipstick for years. At least it is better than starting a new job. Now that is scary.

- The boss who won't listen to your ideas can give you acne and psoriasis. He is probably too important and busy to hear your suggestions. Besides, what's a little chronic skin condition characterized by inflamed, red, raised areas that develop silvery scales, compared to the important stuff he has to deal with?

- The insulting, backstabbing department head can weaken your immune system, making you more vulnerable to colds and minor infections as well as major diseases. Actually saying something to this department head might make him mad, so you can put up with a few major diseases.

- Your incompetent partner, who also happens to be the boss's nephew, can shovel enough stress your way to give you headaches and even panic attacks. Rather than confront the obvious, you would rather take aspirin and run your car into the occasional telephone pole.

- The "fight or flight" response elicited by the promotion of the twenty-three-year-old recent college graduate—your new boss—has raised your blood glucose levels, making it harder to control your diabetes. I hope that this unjust promotion will not cost you your foot or leg. If it does, your new twenty-three-year-old boss will probably send his secretary over with a condolence card. He is thoughtful like that.

- The coworker who continually steals your cost-savings ideas and always refuses to share credit can provide enough stress to give you a good case of insomnia or depression. You had a good idea on how to rig up a hose to your car exhaust, but he would probably steal that too. Standing up to him might cause you social embarrassment. Carbon monoxide may be the easier route.

- Since 1993, the Bureau of Labor Statistics has recorded more than eight hundred workplace homicides per year. How many of these homicides at work do you suppose were stress-related? You have now moved from being really sick and suffering from possibly life-threatening conditions to pennies-on-your-eyes, graveyard dead.

We all have stress in our lives. Every single one of us who is above ground is going to have stress at home and at work. It is unavoidable, unstoppable, and unjust. You can't simply close your eyes and make a wish that stress will disappear, (I know. I have tried.)

The first thing to realize when attempting to deal with stress is that it doesn't play fair. Life does what it does, and you either accept it, learn from it, and become stronger and wiser, or you don't. The other vitally important aspect of stress that we must recognize is that its impact is directly proportional to our perception. How we perceive stressful situations is the starting place for our coping strategies. Some people handle stress in a healthy way. Others are much more prone to stressful reactions. You have probably known people who have a hard time just getting through the day. They may be predisposed to anxiety. Often, they lack problem-solving abilities and tend to throw their hands in the air every time a potential stressor comes along.

Then there are those whom I truly believe love stress and thrive on the ensuing calamity. We call these people "drama queens" (whether male or female). They would never admit it, but they enjoy turning every stressful situation into a full-blown catastrophe. I can't help these people. If this fits you, I recommend that you skip this chapter and start fretting about why the mail is late and what exactly the government is going to do about it. Then call several friends and get them stirred up, too.

In the preceding chapter, "Run—When to," I mentioned the importance of health and divided it into three distinct areas: physical, mental, and spiritual. Although the areas are distinct, they are interconnected. To use an analogy, the diesel motor (mind) and the tractor tires (physical) are all separately maintained entities bolted to the John Deere (spirit). They are each separate with their own identify, but can operate only when joined together. We must protect this triad if we are to prevent our employers, family, and life in general from turning us into dark cutters.

Since I have already addressed spirituality, I limit myself here to physical and mental health. First off, let's see how we stack up in the physical category. On the ranch, we exercise by working. Pounding fence posts, digging ditches, repairing the corrals, hauling hay: all of these activities provide exercise and, believe it or not, relaxation, in addition to limbering up the joints and using the muscles. However, if you smoke or chew tobacco, you will never achieve the physical state needed to effectively deal with stress. In addition, while a few drinks can be soothing and relaxing, over-indulgence will wreck your fine-tuned physicality, and stress will overwhelm you. Never tolerate drug use in your life or the lives of your loved ones. Although many people use a chemical fix in order to self-medicate, the result is always—let me repeat—always a path to annihilation.

To balance my mental health, I find that a few things work well for me. You will find your own methods. The main point is to examine your life and make a conscious effort to include items or activities that heal, soothe, and enhance your mental state. I might have the body of an Olympian, but if I am the village idiot, stress will have a heyday with me.

The most critical item in mental health and stress is to have a true friend. Blessed are you if you have a friend who assists you in all parts of your life, supports you in every endeavor, and for whom you have deep affection and fervent trust. There is no better stress-reliever in the world than being able to pour your heart out to your best friend. Often, that is the only remedy we need.

Another mental health restorative is having a hobby that you absolutely love. Some may want to call it an interest rather than a hobby, because the word "hobby" tends to trivialize things. When you engage in your hobby, you can get lost for hours; and realize only afterward that the stressors of the day have evaporated.

The next mental health item on my list is to make time every day to read. Set aside two or three hours, seven days a week. Divide your reading between fiction and non-fiction. Like your hobby, a good fiction work will absorb you and remove you from this stressful plane, thereby allowing you time to heal. Non-fiction, on the other hand, will engage your mind with new thoughts and ideas. Many non-fiction books will open you up to new concepts and theories that you will later spend hours thinking about and debating with yourself.

Did I ask if you have a dog? My dog is a Bassett hound named Happy. His name says it all. Need I say more?

Lesson from the Ranch

Avoid being a dark-cutter. Deal with everything and everybody up front and straight on.

CHAPTER
35

Succession

"But I tell you the truth; no prophet is accepted in his own hometown."
Luke 4:24

"I can train a cowboy in a few weeks, but a good horse is hard to replace."
Cowboy Wisdom

Succession planning for a ranch or farm operation follows natural order: usually a son will take the place of the father, who took the place of his father. However, in today's world, children often want to do their own thing and move into the cities. After the death or retirement of the owners, ranches and farms are broken up into pieces and sold as small semi-ranches or subdivided into building sites. Kids nowadays want the instant money rather than the lifestyle. (They will pay good money to work out at a health center but don't want to haul hay.) But that's okay. Don't force succession. The only way for it to work is to follow the natural order. The son or daughter must have an innate love of the lifestyle and the sacrifices it entails. To follow something other than the natural order dishes out misery for everyone.

The business world is no different. Allow the natural order to develop and flourish. Too often, we devise and implement succession plans that—while well-meaning—go against the natural flow. This is why most succession plans sit on the shelf turning yellow with time. They just don't work very well.

Succession planning at the top level of your organization is a party that sends no invitations. Your CEO, CFO, and other large Cs have already chosen their heirs. You may or may not know who it is at first, but if you hang around a while, you will. Indeed, the heirs themselves may not know they are the Chosen Ones until it is close to transition time.

One of the disturbing facts of top management succession is the number of children selected to replace their father after he is gone. This is usually a recipe for disaster. The children who rise to the top of the organization are often ill-prepared for real challenges and adversity. All of their lives, the little emperors have been told they have beautiful clothes. Their natural talents and skills are usually in other areas, but they bend to the will of the family as they grudgingly take their place behind the big desk. Sometimes it works, but I have seen it fail numerous times.

Succession planning at the mid-levels is your concern. If you decide to implement succession planning, make sure it is performed in conjunction with the overall organizational strategic plan. Too often, I have seen stand-alone succession plans which did not dovetail with the strategic plans. This is akin to going horseback riding but forgetting to put on the reins. You can go fast and far, but the direction is up for grabs. Someone looking at you from a distance, such as a stock- holder, will think you are in control, but you know better.

There are three methods to perform your succession planning. The first is the traditional approach, whereby committees select the key positions, while you select and discuss nominees. A list of potential successors is developed, each of whom is given assignments and job enhancements that will prepare them for their future roles. This process is very confidential and doesn't rely on assessments from cus- tomers, peers, or subordinates. It also doesn't include formal performance appraisal and incorporation of a systematic personal career development course. Most businesses use the traditional method. It works fine until already trained key players begin to leave. This throws a wrench into the works.

The second approach we define as integrative; that is, it includes both succession planning and career development. By using systematic processes and elaborate tracking programs, this approach ensures objectivity and consistency. The integra- tive method is future oriented and dovetails with the strategic plan. Built into this approach is the ability to be flexible and responsive to change. The downside is the discipline that is required to operate this system over the long haul. Since it also nullifies the *good ole boy* network, you may find an undercurrent of resistance to this approach.

The third approach to succession planning is the natural order. Okay, I just made up that phrase. However, that is what we will call it anyway. The natural order is simply that: allowing the cream to rise to the top. A lot of this involves just getting out of the way of a talented person or helping to remove roadblocks. The cream will rise; it is just a question of whether it is your quart jar or someone else's. While this approach sounds simple, it takes a manager who is on top of his or her game to pull it off. If this is done right, the manager will instinctively know who stays, who goes, and the reasons. The manager will also have identified the promotable individuals. Bear in mind that this approach is wedded to cross-functionality. In the natural order, there are no departments or areas: a star player in shipping can become a star player in HR management much more easily than the laboriously groomed heir. This approach is all about keeping a sharp eye out for potential. Once potential is identified, the smart person will move this individual among different departments, thus exposing him or her to a broad view of the business. Not only will this build a stronger bench and a future star player, but it will also enrich and enhance this person's work life while avoiding another turnover statistic. So look for the stars. They will be trying to get your attention in all sorts of ways.

Often in succession planning, the question arises of promoting internal versus external talent. Many HR professionals preach about internal promotions but then regularly go outside the organization to fill positions. I have never understood this practice, except to refer once again to the statement Jesus made concerning prophets in their own country. Let us take a quick look at the advantages and disadvantages of internal versus external promotions.

In my mind, the following are the reasons for internal promotions:

- I know what I am getting and what the employee needs to succeed. Outside applicants are often like potted meat. Not only are you hiring outside talent, but you are also hiring the problems that go with the applicant.

- It is much less expensive. Usually, salaries have to be a bit higher to attract an outsider. In addition, there is the added expense of recruiter fees (twenty to thirty percent), relocation charges, and initial orientation time. The hidden costs of hiring outside the organization are astronomical.

- Training on the organization's specific policies takes much longer with an external hire. More importantly, it takes considerable time to learn and engrain the corporate culture. Often the external hire cannot adapt to a specific culture, so the process must start anew.

There are also definite advantages of external staffing. For me, the defined advantages are in the following three areas:

- You need fresh eyes and ears. The internal person is so used to the way things are that he or she doesn't see the potential changes that could help the organization improve services, reduce waste, improve morale, and so on.

- There is a larger labor market to tap for talent. When you recruit outside the organization, you cast a much wider net in your search for special-ized occupations and professions. In fact, many skills you may need are simply not available in your organization. An internal person may be a great person, with a fantastic attitude and sharp intellect, but if he is not a master machinist and that's what you need, you are barking up the wrong tree.

- External hires can drastically help in creating a more diverse workforce. Sometimes, it is simply not possible or feasible to fill positions with internal applicants while ensuring your organiza-tion reflects your population. If you find yourself in this predicament, by all means, go outside to recruit. You will be glad you did.

With this said, I strongly advocate internal promotions if possible. The advantages in morale alone outweigh the disadvantages. Morale equals profit. This is very plain and simple. Perhaps most importantly, internal promotions come without hidden problems. Of course they will have problems—we all do—but at least we are not eating potted meat.

On the ranch, we use the natural order to determine which bull will mate with the cattle. Bulls that are successful in mating are engaged in succession planning. They are planning for their DNA to move into the next generation. To decide which bull mates, we let them fight. My method is to use an odd number of bulls. While two are fighting, the odd man out will be breeding. This is not so much survival of the fittest as survival of the smartest.

On a cattle ranch, the rancher needs replacement heifers every now and then, to replace heifers that have died or become infertile. In this endeavor, you can recruit from outside, or purchase, replacement heifers or mama cows. It costs a lot, and you don't really know what you are getting, but it is a way to fix your problem. Alternatively, you can take the smart approach and breed your own replacement heifers. Sure, it takes a little more time and some light planning, but you know exactly what you are getting, and the expense and risk are minimal compared to external purchases. There will be times when you will need fresh genetics, but that is the exception, not the norm, especially if you already have good bloodlines.

The lesson from the ranch is to breed your own heifers. (I would caution you choose another term for your employees.) I will be even more specific, and suggest that your internal promotion to external hire ratio should be five to one. There you have it. Have fun stargazing.

Lesson from the Ranch

Don't buy another man's problems. Raise your own stock to ensure quality.

CHAPTER
36

Teamwork

"Share each other's burdens, and in this way obey the law of Christ. If you think you are too important to help someone, you are only fooling yourself. You are not that important."
Galatians 6:2 - 3

"The strength of the ranch is the cowboy. The strength of the cowboy is the ranch."
Cowboy Wisdom

I am not going to expound on the virtues of teamwork. Anyone who has survived the third grade knows the value of collective thought and effort. The focus of this chapter will be on improvement of teamwork. The goal is to subordinate individual interests to team unity and effectiveness. The most important lesson I ever learned about teamwork came from Captain Kangaroo, a children's show which aired weekday mornings on CBS from 1955 until 1984. In the Captain's story about Stone Soup, three soldiers arrive at a small village, carrying nothing more than a large empty pot. They go door to door asking for food. As food is scarce in their mountain valley, the villagers are unwilling to share. All over the village, doors are slammed. Undaunted, the soldiers fill the pot with water, drop a large stone in it, and place it over a fire in the village square. One of the villagers becomes curious and asks what they are doing. The soldiers answer that they are making "stone soup," which tastes wonderful, although it still needs some carrots to improve the flavor. The villager doesn't mind parting with his carrots to help them out. Another villager walks by, inquiring about the pot, and the soldiers again mention their stone soup which could use some onion. The villager rushes back to his house and returns with the onion. More and more villagers walk by, each adding another ingredient. Finally, a delicious pot of soup is enjoyed by all. I learned this as a kid, but even today when I see people voluntarily coming together to achieve a greater good, I think of Stone Soup. If you want to get people to do something, don't beg and plead. Instead, create the impression that you are giving them the opportunity to be part of your success,

The high times of the storied cattle drives lasted about twenty years. From the end of the Civil War until around the mid-1880s, cowboys drove an estimated 10 million head of cattle from Texas to the railheads of Kansas and Missouri. Some were herded even further north to be used as breeding stock in Wyoming and Canada. A tiny herd might have only five hundred head of cattle, while the biggest herds had around fifteen thousand. To accomplish this massive feat, a cattle baron would hire cowboys at a ratio of one cowboy for every two hundred fifty to four hundred head of cattle. The cowboys faced hostile Indians and even hostile settlers who would shoot at them for crossing their land. They fought swollen rivers, sinkholes, hailstorms, and drought. The next stampede was always just over the rise. There was never enough water for the cattle and never enough sleep for the men.

We often think of cowboys as rugged individualists. This is simply not so. Without robust teamwork, the entire cattle drive would have fallen apart within the first few days. Instead, success was the norm, and failure the extreme exception. As with any organization, the cowboy trail team had positions, many of which rotated on a daily basis. The wrangler took care of the extra horses. Several people rode flank (back), swing (front), and point (front). The man assigned to drag (rear) rode behind the herd, pushing the cattle forward and picking up stragglers. (If you ever wondered if the kerchiefs the cowboys wore around their necks were really needed, you only have to ride drag one day to find out.) Ahead rode the cook and the trail boss. Often, there would be a scout riding far ahead to pick out the best route and to ensure that the trail was safe and passable.

Outside of the cook and trail boss, most of the positions were interchangeable. In a pinch, one of the cowboys could replace even the cook on the trail, but you would quickly discover that you wouldn't need any of the new fad diets. Some cowboys could scout or wrangle horses better than others. However, for the most part, this formidable team could overcome any obstacle. No matter the position, everyone played his role without complaint. The cowboys bonded on the long trail, and many would seek each other out on future cattle drives so they could ride together again with people they trusted. In addition, as you will remember from a previous chapter, this was a racially diverse group with radically different backgrounds and cultures.

Do your teams work as well as the cowboys did? Could you take just twenty of your managers and have them drive eight thousand head of cattle from the Rio Grande to South Dakota? Is the visual now rattling around in your head? I will be the first to confess that I have never developed a team that could pull this off. Nevertheless, it doesn't keep me from trying. Let's take a hard look at what they had that our modern organizations don't. Maybe some of these differences will give us pause when we try to engage people in teamwork.

The cowboys had no organizational chart. Except for the trail boss and the cook, everyone was on the same level. All positions, whether it was riding flank or point, were equally important. No one was trying to make his position seem superior to the others. Why should they? They were all cross-trained in the various tasks. Without ladder rungs within the team, the cowboy didn't waste his time jockeying to move up the ladder, and he didn't have to be concerned about moving down the ladder. The next time we form a team, we need to stress that when we function as a team, regardless of individual titles, we are all equal.

The same pay went to each cowboy: $30 a month and food. The trail boss usually received one hundred dollars a month, and the cook was somewhere in the middle. You didn't receive merit increases, and you never had your pay reduced. You pulled your weight, and you received your pay at the end of the drive. Cowboys didn't have an entry-level point, a mid-point, or a maximum. Often, they would receive bonuses paid for various incentives, such as number of live head delivered or arriving on time. If the bonus was paid, it was paid to all equally.. How does that compare with your organization?

The cowboys shared the same risks. The toil and trouble that existed on the open range was borne by each cowboy. Each day, someone could be killed by gunshot, arrow, or stampede. Each day, they risked bad food and bad water. The downpour and the bone-chilling wind hit all of them with the same ferocity. Are the risks the same for all of your team members? Do some reside in a safe harbor, escaping the elements? In today's environment, we stick some people in piddling jobs, where their fawning and kowtowing ways protect them from harm, and others we push into incredibly hard jobs where the failure rate is high. The ones who don't possess political skills find themselves jobless and penniless. Is this sharing the risk? Does it rain on the just and the unjust? What do you think?

The cowboys had a single well-defined goal: to deliver live cattle to a specified place at a specified time. There were no tangents, no individual interests, and no manager coming in at the last hour changing the objective. They had a simple common goal. Everyone knew the goal and could recite it by heart. Each morning, the cowboys reminded themselves of the common goal and did everything in their power to ensure that the team achieved that day's target. How well defined are our team's goals? Can everyone recite the goal? Does everyone know his or her part? Is the team's goal simple or so complex it takes a three-ring binder? (A common problem is not a goal.) Once the goal is achieved, the team no longer has a reason to exist, and should be disbanded. This doesn't always happen ,,, which is rather like reaching your destination in Dodge City, and then to keep driving the cattle into Alberta. Sounds silly, doesn't it? but that is what we often do.

The cowboys handled individual grievances immediately and then moved on. Problems between cowboys did not fester and spread among the team. If a disagreement arose, someone would quickly relent his position. If not, a good friendly fistfight would resolve the problem. Pounding someone in the head often produces a clearer view of the problem. I am not advocating workplace violence (which is what they call it today), but individual team members must be able to work out their differences in short order. To do otherwise taints the entire team, even to the extent of choosing sides. This is not teamwork. It is a battle. Warring soldiers never drove eight thousand head of cattle anywhere. I have personally disrupted many teams in the past years by wanting to 'have my way.' I hope that you will do much better than I have.

The trail boss fired the cowboy who could not or would not become part of the team. Without ceremony or prerequisite activity, they cut him loose. While rare, some wannabe cowboys never managed to become part of the team. In that event, the trail boss wouldn't draw out the corrective action process. Once he saw that the others had turned against this individual, the trail boss would cut the cowboy loose near the next settlement. The trail boss didn't issue a verbal warning, take progressive disciplinary action, or call his law firm. He didn't counsel with the cattle baron or take written statements. The trail boss fired the cowboy and fired him fast. His gut instinct told him what to do. He knew that unless he took quick action, the cowboys would be letting him know clearly what should be done. Do you have members of the team who 'don't play well with others'? Do you know what to do about it?

To run a team in today's modern corporate world using the cowboys as a model is extreme. However, maybe the cowboys knew something we have forgotten. The next time you form a team, I hope you are thinking, *head 'em up, move 'em out*.

Lesson from the Ranch

Only fools and a few outlaws operate alone.

CHAPTER 37

Training

"Instruct the wise and they will be even wiser. Teach the righteous,
and they will learn even more."
Proverbs 9:9

"Generally, you ain't learnin' nothing when your mouth's a-jawin'."
Cowboy Wisdom

A new, radical method of horse training has arisen in recent years. Rather than using strong-arm and even brutal tactics, men and women who train horses (and other animals) have embraced the concept of the "horse whisperer," a trainer who develops an individual training model which focuses on the motives and desires of the horse. While many believe this to be a New Age departure in animal training, in fact the term goes back to the early nineteenth century when an Irish horseman, Daniel Sullivan (who died in AD 1810), achieved a bit of fame by rehabilitating horses that had become vicious and out of control due to accidental trauma or abuse. He kept his methods and techniques secret. Through the years, various trainers have rediscovered and revived his system. Today, trainers use animal psychology at all the top-tier animal training schools. Have you ever seen a performance of the Spanish Riding School of Vienna, Austria? Is it not amazing what the Lipizzaner stallions can accomplish? For more than four hundred years, the Spanish Riding School has used firm, yet gentle, techniques that result in an obedient and calm horse.

Even further back in history, an Athenian warrior and author, Xenophon, was known as the first "horse whisperer." His teacher, Socrates, molded much of Xenophon's thinking. As an expert in the training of warhorses, Xenophon believed in sympathetic horsemanship. His methods of training warhorses involved positive reinforcement, extreme patience, and understanding of horse psychology. In addition, he advocated creating a strong bond between man and animal so that the horse would respond because it liked and respected the man on its back, not due to a whip. To read his "On Horsemanship," written in 322 BC, is like reading a modern dissertation on employee training and development.

Why have I spent so much time discussing dressage? The answer is uncomplicated and basic. In our employee training, we must become "people whisperers." As I reflect back on the years of training I have attended, performed, developed, and witnessed, I would estimate eighty percent of it to have been a waste of time and effort. This number may seem high to you. Surely, we have performed better than this, you say. However, I would challenge you to reflect on your own organization's training success. American corporations spend billions of dollars annually on employee training, yet a lot of it is not effective. Here are a few of the reasons.

- We fail to base training on *needs assessments* that tie into the strategic plan. This is coupled to an uncertainty as to what skills actually are needed to perform the task effectively. A true needs assessment costs time and money. Indeed, such an assessment requires a lot of intellectual grease.

- In most cases the training is not relevant to a person's job. Just throw everybody in the room and train them together—surely, someone needs it. This is easier than actually developing a target audience. How many of these misguided types of training sessions have you had to endure in your career?

- We fail to consider aptitude when we design training, which results in the training being either too comprehensive or too basic. You will either struggle to keep up or fall asleep.

- Training doesn't follow sound practice. We will discuss this later in-depth.

- Training is not a management priority. Training is simply not exciting to upper management. It would take another chapter to cover this area. For now, just trust me; training is not something high on their priority lists.

- Training is never, repeat never, allotted the needed time. It is always allotted either too much time or not enough. This relates back to sound practice.

- There is an over-reliance on trial-and-error learning or on-the-job training. How many of you learned to swim by your dad throwing you off the dock? It worked for Dad. Why do my results differ from Dad's results?

- There is an assumption by managers that their new employees already possess the necessary job skills. This works only for brides.

- We have a lack of qualified internal trainers. Unless you are conducting training in astrophysics, you probably have all the skills and abilities you need in-house. Develop your own trainers. It is the best money you will ever spend.

- Some managers depend on external trainers who, at the end of the day, could not care less whether you succeed or fail. They are worried about getting back home or if the check cleared.

- We have an insufficient training budget. Forgot the needs assessment and forgot to set money aside?

So how do we repair this expensive, bloated, ineffectual training system we have inherited from our ancestors in the business world? First, I suggest you directly relate training to the mission statement, the strategic plan, and the standing plan. If your training curriculum doesn't connect to your mission statement, strategic plan, or standing plans, there is a good chance that you really don't need to train, or even that you have your dog barking up the wrong tree. This is step one. Review with a fine-toothed comb.

Choosing the right audience sounds like a simple endeavor; however, we hardly ever get it right. In many training sessions, you have a few who really would benefit more from a synopsis or a quick email rather than the full-blown course. As you choose your audience, try to get away from the group or department mindset. Training the wrong person not only wastes your time and the company's money, but it also aggravates the person you have at gunpoint.

As a whole, we all developed our training model after old Mrs. Snodgrass in the third grade. She was the teacher, you were the pupil, and you had better sit there and be quiet as she droned on about the ABCs. Adult learners are quite different. Unlike third-graders, most adults see themselves as responsible for their own decisions and lives. Adults need to know *why* they need to learn something. In addition, each class may have a wide variety of ages in attendance. People in their fifties, sixties, and seventies can learn new techniques and acquire new knowledge just as well as younger people, but, much as it hurts me, I will be the first to confess that the older ones will need a little more time. When you have a broad mix of ages in your training class, you will have some who are bored and some who are struggling. Be aware of this and come up with creative solutions.

To become "people whisperers," we have to fine-tune our observation skills to accurately determine the adult learner's aptitude. This includes leadership ability, skills, talents, capacity, and overall potential. I often start a new training course with an exercise in survival. Whether it is in the desert or the Cascade Mountains, I place the attendees into a simulated life-and-death situation and then observe how they work in teams in their attempts to remain alive. Not only do they begin the course learning the value of teamwork (team scores always exceed individual scores), but it provides an unparalleled opportunity for me to closely observe the aptitude of each participant. Armed with this knowledge, I can then customize on the spot the type of teaching methods I will use. As I tend to have interactive training sessions, I team people up to bring forth the synergy. Also based on the observations in the survival situation, I often keep a select few "after school" for more intensive training.

If your organization gives only lip service to the value of training, you have a real problem. If learning is not a high priority for management, people will sense that training is not valued and react in kind. While you may not be able to change the culture of upper management, you can use a simple technique to help to dispel this mindset and increase the employee's satisfaction in training. At the beginning of each training session, regardless of what kind of training is involved, have a member of upper management introduce the course objective, course curriculum, and the instructor, and at the same time voice his or her support for the training. This sets the tone for the training and shows that it is valued. If your management team resists this idea and cannot be bothered to invest five minutes of their time, it is time for you to seek employment elsewhere. You obviously work for a self-important idiot. Unless you wish to become one yourself, you need to flee.

On-the-job (OTJ) training is also called trial-and-error training. A little of this goes a long way and is a valuable piece of the overall learning process. Regretfully, sometimes the only training we provide to new people is OTJ. We push them out of the boat, and if they don't swim right off the bat, we beat them over the head with the boat paddle. After several disciplinary warnings (beatings), they slowly slip under the surface. After they drown (terminated), we complain about the sorry state of the applicant pool. What an idiot the last person was. Of course, I have never done anything like this. I have also never told a lie. Can you see my nose growing?

I have always been a huge advocate of developing in-house trainers. This has several distinct advantages. The clearest advantage is how easy it is to conduct follow-up evaluation and possible retraining with your own in-house trainer. Another strong reason is the passion an in-house trainer will bring to the classroom, as opposed to someone you have simply hired. The in-house trainer will also be able to customize the courses to what will actually be needed. Most of the trainers for hire can only provide their companies' canned presentations. My last main reason for "train the trainer" modus operandi is that it is an excellent tool to use in developing your management team and plans for succession. The time, effort, and difficult gyrations an in-house trainer must undergo allows you to separate the wheat from the chaff. Talk about a win/win situation.

I have had some of the worst training experiences that a person could tolerate. I have also had the best training experience, and this was on the ranch. Everything I know about cattle and running a ranch, I learned at the knee of my father. I made a truckload of mistakes while I learned. Yet Dad would never criticize or belittle. He would usually just get a good laugh out of my incompetence. In addition, while his training mode was easy-going, it was firm. I spent several nights out in the cold rain fixing the mistakes he had laughed about that afternoon. No, Dad wouldn't let me off the hook without consequences. He wanted me to be responsible for my own actions or inactions. After being away from the rural life for many years, I was deeply surprised at the amount of knowledge and skill I had retained after those long years. A torrent of memories rain down as my son and I perform our farm work. It is very comforting to hear my father's voice gently guiding me in my tasks. Maybe someday, after I am gone, my son will hear my voice. I like to think he will.

Lesson from the Ranch

To truly prosper, learn to be a people whisperer.

Turnover

"The human spirit can endure a sick body,
but who can bear a crushed spirit?"
Proverbs 18:14

"Only a dang fool will lose a good job, a good horse, or a good woman."
Cowboy Wisdom

Here is a bit of ranching knowledge that everyone who has worked on a ranch or farm knows to be an ultimate truth. A cow or a bull can leave your pasture anytime the animal wants to. It doesn't matter how much money you spent on your fancy fencing, if they get it in their heads to bolt for "greener pastures," they will. Don't get me wrong: good fences are imperative. However, I have seen one thousand two hundred-pound cows jump over five-foot-high fences, cows lift up the fence and pull the posts out of the ground, and bulls looking for a fight simply walk through five strands of tight, barbed wire. The wires will sing as they snap across the bull's chest.

Usually, it takes an "event" to spark a cow's desire to leave the pasture. However, often it is just a strong desire to explore. Hard-wired in the bovine's DNA is a natural instinct to roam. They are range animals and need the wide-open spaces. Their naturally curious minds want to see what kind of forage is over the hill.

You have to ask yourself why they don't escape more often. The sad fact is that cattle do get out a lot more than people think. As a matter of fact, I don't know of a single rancher who hasn't had to drive the roads looking for an escapee. Through the years, I have had to search for the wanderlust-stricken beasts myself. This whole issue can be very expensive to the rancher. Besides the emotional price you pay, sometimes you never get the cattle back. Sometimes they wind up sold on someone else's ranch. Sometimes, predators kill the cattle. Sometimes, vehicles kill animals on the highways. All kinds of incidents can happen. The bottom line is that you have to replace valuable animals. The replacement heifers or bulls will come to you as an unknown, full of unpleasant surprises. They may bring new diseases into your herd. As newcomers, they will be more apt to find the weak points in your fences. They may or may not be productive and breed as they should. Their bloodlines may be suspicious (pig in a poke), and they may produce inferior calves. The herd doesn't readily accept them and can sometimes become aggressive, resulting in injuries to both newcomer and existing herd. You will also have to spend much of your valuable time socializing the animals. I could go on and on, but I have probably over-stressed the point.

Turnover in your organization and escaping cattle on a ranch are the same problem. Moreover, some of the basic solutions for the ranch might just work for the organization. Is there enough grass, hay, grain, and water to meet the basic needs? This is the same as asking if the employees are really making enough compensation to meet their basic needs. Under-fed cattle and under-paid employees will both fix their eyes on the horizon and start searching for improvement in feed or cash. I know that it is extremely popular nowadays to quote "polls" that indicate money is not a big factor. In many jobs, I am sure that is true. However, the positions at the bottom of the food chain don't buy into this new "money is not important" paradigm. There is a colossal difference between $5.16 an hour and $10 an hour. Some people might think, *That's only $10K a year difference. That's not a lot of money.* They are right when we are discussing people with six-figure salaries. Now, I am not advocating we go out and raise salaries blindly. Nevertheless, we should be paying what is fair and equitable for the region and industry.

With that said, it sickens me to know that there are certain business models that keep their rate at or near the federal minimum to encourage high turnover. It is their unspoken policy that high turnover keeps everyone from "topping out," thereby saving vast amounts in salaries. High turnover also greatly reduces the organization's insurance expenses, since most employees quit before reaching eligibility. To avoid litigation, I would never name the organizations that engage in this sleazy practice. Suffice it to say, they need to examine their corporate values and strive to do the right thing.

All managers know that turnover is expensive. However, as managers, we have not done our jobs very well. Ask any managers if they believe turnover is costly, and they will start sputtering and slinging words — yet not be able to quantify the estimated costs. Don't believe me? Go out and survey your top managers. If you research this area, you will find a wide array of answers ranging from the ridiculously low to the outrageously high, from only ten percent up to two hundred percent of annual compensation. The hidden costs are more difficult to estimate and include customer service disruption, emotional costs, loss of morale, burnout/absenteeism among remaining employees, loss of experience, loss of continuity, loss of "corporate memory," workers' compensation expenses, relocation costs, interview time, advertising, recruitment fees, lowered quality standards, poor community image, to cite only a few factors. Indeed, I don't believe you can ever capture all of the true costs of turnover. At best, it is only going to be an educated guesstimate. I personally like the one-third rule: that is, turnover costs about a third of the annual salary of the person you are replacing. This is probably too low, but we have to start somewhere.

Once you are sure you have the organization's compensation, benefits, and other rewards in line with competing organizations, it is time to look at the root causes of why nameplates change continually. We are willing accomplices when we succumb to pressure to hire fast. The quick fix is to stick to your principles and continue to hire slow. If you are strong-armed into hiring fast despite your protestations, you need to add to the growing turnover numbers by quitting yourself.

Another no-brainer is offering flextime and granting time off to take care of personal issues. Unless you have just fallen off a turnip truck, you are aware of the importance today's workers place on a balanced life. I firmly believe that we are heading in the right direction when we consciously evaluate our employees' life balance. Back in the days when our culture was agriculturally driven, we maintained our life balance by the very nature of our friends and family oriented working lives. In the twentieth century, we lost the balance that we have had for thousands of years. Only recently have people been discussing a return to balance. The reason is straightforward. Without this God-given balance, we no longer have a true purpose, real happiness, or an inner calmness. Instead, we think our true purpose is to enrich Mr. Scrooge while climbing over the bloodied backs of our coworkers as we scramble up the corporate ladder. How sad. If you truly want to lower turnover, try throwing the employees a little balance. In the end, this balance will continue to line the pockets of Mr.

Scrooge, and you will make it up that ladder without the blood. (They claim there is a nice view from the top rung. I also understand it hurts a whole lot more when you fall. It has something to do with terminal velocity.)

Once we get past the basic stuff like compensation and the no-brainers such as job fit, we can finally focus on the true cause of the greatest percentage of turnover. The solution is simple to implement, virtually cost-free, and has already been acknowledged by everyone with an IQ over 60. Briefly, let the employees know how their roles fit in with the bigger picture and how important they are to the success of the team. We know that people are social beings. This is why we cluster together in cities. We join clubs and associations for the social aspects rather than the charter purpose. For the most part, people attend church for social reasons, especially to have others see them in attendance. Attendance socially validates that they really are good people. In experiments with Internet voting (don't fight the traffic and crowds; vote at home in your robe), it has been found that voter participation actually dropped. It seems people like to gather around the polling places. Like attending church, being witnessed voting socially validates that you are a good citizen.

People want to be a part of something bigger. They want to know that their vote counts, and just as importantly, they want everyone to know that they perform their civic duty. The workplace should follow this guide. When we bring on board newly hired people, we should spend time telling them how they fit into the broader scope. Do we show them how their positions are critical to the overall success of the organization? More likely than not, we simply take them to their work areas and say, "This is your job." Obviously, the tasks they perform are critical to our success; otherwise we wouldn't have created them. Do we tell the stonecutter that he is building a majestic cathedral? On the other hand, do we tell him his job is to cut the stone to specifications? A few words can make a big difference.

Before I leave this subject, I would like to point out that I have considered conducting formalized exit surveys with the cattle that decide to leave the ranch. On second thought, I realized this is not a good idea. In addition to their inability to speak or write (as far as I know—I cannot say what happens after I leave the field), if I sit real quiet and watch them closely for a few hours, I can readily figure out why they want to leave. The answers are always grossly evident. Can we not do this with our employees?

Lesson from the Ranch

A world class fence won't hold an unhappy bull.

Value

"They are always thinking about how much it costs. 'Eat and drink,' they say, but they don't mean it."
Proverbs 23:7

"What price do you place on a crisp mountain morning?"
Cowboy Wisdom

Money should not be the driving factor in our lives. However, to survive in the big leagues, we must learn to think, act, and communicate in terms of money. Our corporate leadership understands money and often nothing else. The boss is built this way, and it is through this process that he or she has advanced and is now your boss. So if you want to do well in your career or even survive the next few years, you must become adept at monetary speak.

It is all very simple. If our organization doesn't make enough money to satisfy its various needs, it will wither and die. Through the years, human-related activity has come to be seen as a burden on the company's bottom line. Indeed, the costs related to this item have been tagged as unavoidable. (I have actually heard this term used in a top-level meeting.) I know and you know that this is not the real truth. In fact, while we don't actually handle or produce the product or services, the human factor is a major player in the profitability of our companies. The problem is one of perception. We spend all of our time holding the box together while failing to show upper management the actual value of human factors to the company. We aren't accountants or bankers. Some of you may have backgrounds in finance or possess an MBA, but for the most part, we simply go about our tasks with little thought to the monthly profit and loss statement.

To gain a real picture of the value of managing people, quantify it. In earlier decades, anything to do with managing people was viewed as activity-based: we hire, we fire, we pay, we track trends, we insure. Today, people management has shifted to a results-based approach. Because management has made a sizable investment in our existence, it becomes a duty to show a return on investment (ROI). That is a very easy thing to say, and for most areas within an organization, it is a relatively easy thing to do. With people management, showing an ROI is a much harder process. People management does deal in a few areas that, with a little hard work, can be quantified: such as turnover expense, absenteeism costs, costs of hiring, or EEOC fines. Even within these relatively simple quantifiable areas, however, we often have a credibility problem. The numbers we plug into our formulas are often nebulous.

Measuring the financial impact of the so-called *soft* side of people management is our biggest credibility problem. By *soft* side, I mean things such as culture, diversity, complaints, creativity, leadership, ethics, customer satisfaction, effective teamwork, conflict resolution. We know that the programs and processes we create and implement add value, even tremendous value, to the organization. Our problem is determining how much value, in a way that others can appreciate. When we do find a way to measure and assign monetary value, our leaders rightfully question the validity of our data. They view our data as being too assumption-based and driven by wild guesses. They daydream through our presentations and twiddle their thumbs while waiting to get to the production and accounting people so they can tell our leaders what is really going on. They will sometimes even feign excitement at our charts in an effort to be nice, but they don't mean it.

How do we fix this problem? One way to get management buy-in on the numbers and data we are generating is to take the baloney out of the sandwich and replace it with choice rib eye steak (preferably Angus). Use your next face-to-face time discussing the methodologies your department uses in generating calculations to determine the value of various areas. The leadership will want to change some of your calculations and almost certainly will want to question the numbers – but that is fantastic. By allowing them leeway in the formulation construction, you automatically have buy-in to the validity of the data you present. That was easy.

Along with this process, you will want to eliminate fuzzy words from your vocabulary when making your next presentation. Upper management is used to hearing HR managers use vague and imprecise speech. Accustomed to the business-driven, stark language of the boardroom, leaders are too often confronted by HR people who don't use the language of numbers but rather the language of sixth graders: *tremendous* savings, *huge* reductions, *fantastic* results These words are fine if we decide to have a group hug or become a used car salesperson, but leave them out of the boardroom.

Next, let's place a monetary value on everything we do. Many experts will tell you this is neither possible nor desirable. I say bull butter. There is money attached to everything we do. Even sitting at home alone watching TV and eating corn chips has a cost. Someone has to pay for the chips. The couch was not free. The TV has depreciation value. The power company certainly charges for electricity. Then there is the price you pay when your wife comes home and you don't have the yard mowed. You see, everything has a price tag. It is up to the clever, creative mind to develop the formulations that will give us the monetary impact of the *soft* side of people management.

Take conflict, for example. The declining number of complaints can measure the level of conflict reduction. This may be an internal peer review process, an 800-number reporting line, or a union grievance process. The number of these conflicts or complaints is trackable. In turn, the number and cost of OFCCP, EEOC charges, lawsuits, wage and hour disputes, and arbitrations are trackable. As the number of conflict complaints rise, they will be a linear rise in litigation costs. Any change in one or the other is exactly proportional to change in the other. So X number of conflicts during X period at location A equals X number of EEOC claims. This will give you a ratio of conflicts to claims. To calculate the cost of EEOC claims, you must count all hours spent on the case by you, your staff, or others in your organization, the legal fees you may have paid, all transportation and preparation, and, finally, any mediated settlement. To this number, add the amount of internal time spent investigating conflicts and complaints. Try to capture every hidden cost. If you use an 800-number reporting system, remember the 800-number services have a monthly fee. Continue this exercise until you have captured the cost of all arbitrations, lawsuits, and every cost you can track. Now it becomes a simple matter of backing the number of conflicts into this total number, thereby giving you a cost per conflict. At your next staff meeting, you can now talk about the success of your recent initiative, which has reduced conflict by thirty percent, saving the organization $210,000. Now you have shown a ROI, and

now you have a seat at the table. You can also justify request-
ing an increase in your budget. This is better than begging and
waiting for crumbs.

Use the above process for everything you do. It is a
lot of upfront hard work, but it can be fun, too, as you
suddenly see the true value of your hard work. What someone
does in HR management is every bit as valuable (and often
more so) as the other departments. We just have to prove it. In
addition, remember, have fun with it.

Lesson from the Ranch

Everything you do has investment value. Prove it.

40

Words

"Kind words are like honey—sweet to the soul and healthy for the body."
Proverbs 16:24

"You can't unsay a cruel word."
Cowboy Wisdom

Words on the ranch are rare. Moreover, when some one is talking, there is usually a point. This limited use of words probably developed because most of a rancher's time is spent with beasts that cannot talk back. I think they are sometimes surprised when we humans do talk back.

As we know, there are many uses for words. On the ranch, words are just for pure communication. In the workplace, we obviously use words for much more than conveying our thoughts and ideas. We use kind words as tools and cruel words as weapons. When I say cruel, I mean words intended to inflict harm or belittle somebody. The words by themselves are not considered cruel, but their aim is dark and evil. Kind words and cruel words: together, these words don't constitute yin and yang, in that they are not equal and necessary for harmony. Some misguided people think that way, but they are wrong. There is never a reason to use harsh words.

As a management professional, you need to help people within your organization recognize and avoid harsh words. This is a target-rich environment, since we encounter their usage every day. Unfortunately, for the most part we turn a deaf ear and walk away, pretending we did not hear the assault. It is commonplace to hear words in the workplace used to embarrass, humiliate, and belittle fellow associates or subordinates. This is nothing but a power trip that should cease. How many times have you seen someone embarrass or humiliate his or her boss in front of other people? That is correct. You have never seen that happen. Therefore, this type of usage is a power thing.

Our ancient laws forbid verbally oppressing a widow or an orphan. I believe that rule should extend to hurting anyone with words; the laws having highlighted widows and orphans only because they are the most commonly recognized sufferers. In fact, all people suffer; and so we should guard our words and carefully measure them before letting them loose into the world. Most people are living lives full of private pain, pain they hide from us and from the world. Do we add to their distress with our flippant use of harsh words? Henry David Thoreau said, "The mass of men lead lives of quiet desperation and go to the grave with the song still in them." Do we add to this desperation by using words to taunt and bring anger? Do we use our repertoire of weapons to discourage and undermine and to stifle the 'song still in them'? If we look in our hearts, we know the answer. Heaven forbid that I didn't have the courage to step up to the plate and confess my sins. I would *like* to think that my days of intimidating and controlling others with my words are over. What I really think is that I, like most people, am a work in progress. By helping others recognize their use of words as harmful weapons, maybe I can help myself.

Mother Theresa said, "Kind words may be short … but their echoes are endless." The power of kind words is one of the most amazing things on God's green earth. I know this to be one of the few ultimate truths. Kind words spoken at the correct time have changed lives for the better. It could be those who have sprung their last spring. It might be someone who is not just at the bottom of the barrel but lives under the dang thing. Kind words not only change lives, they save lives. Using kind words is the least expensive gift we can give and takes so little effort, yet it has immense power.

When we use kind words to correct a person's behavior, the result is usually positive. Compared to the harsh words we usually use in our disciplinary actions, kind words get the job done much faster and with longer-lasting results. As a bonus, using kind words makes us better people. As a people, we all have an innate desire to follow the Law of Nature, the law of knowing the difference between Right and Wrong, which C.S. Lewis labels the Moral Law. Choosing kind words where others would often choose harsh words satisfies our inner need to do the right thing. With kind words, we can effectively lead, guide and teach. With kind words, we sleep soundly through the night, and our 'students' excel beyond our wildest dreams.

When I was twelve years old, Dad was letting me drive the pickup truck around on the farm. One day, he let me drive back to the house as he rode in the passenger seat. I was as drawn up as a cat about to be baptized. I safely maneuvered through a couple of tight spots. I was approaching my last obstacle, which was a fourteen-foot gate opening with crossties set on each side. All I had to do was to guide a truck that was only five feet wide through this gate. You would think this gave me a sufficiently large error margin. Well, nine feet of clearance was not enough. I ran smack dab into the crosstie on the right. The impact jarred us only a little bit, but it did some real damage to the front of the truck. I could tell this by the jet of steam shooting up from the grillwork. I sat there in stone-cold silence, awaiting the wrath of Father to descend on me. I just knew I was going to get it good. I was just praying the punishment wouldn't take too long, as it was close to dinnertime and I was hungry. Finally, after a silence that seemed to last for weeks, Dad said, "Next time, aim for the middle." I slowly gave him a sideways glance and saw that he was smiling. I could tell he wanted to laugh, but the extra expense I had just incurred probably kept him from doing so. We walked home in silence. Dad was probably thinking about the repair bill; I was thinking of my enormous relief. Before we walked into the house to relay the good news to mom, Dad turned to me and said, "Don't worry about it, son, those kind of things just happen." I spent some time later in life wondering why Dad never got after me for wrecking his truck. Then I finally realized that I was just learning to drive, and harsh words would not have fixed the truck or improved my driving skills. To use harsh words toward me would have just been venting anger. Now, Mom's reaction was another story ...

Lesson from the Ranch

The most painful and long-lasting wounds are those inflicted by words.

CHAPTER
41

Wrap Up

"The grace of the Lord Jesus be with you all."
Revelations 22:21

"If you continue to ride off into the sunset,
you'll ultimately wind up in the Pacific Ocean."
Cowboy Wisdom

Here we are at the Pacific Ocean, the end of our management journey. In the preceding chapters, I have made an effort at bonding the work ethics and values that are evident in rural America with the practice of managing people. Sometimes, it was an easy matter, and the two slipped together in a seamless blend. At other times, it was more a difficult task requiring a shoehorn and WD-40, but in the end, we achieved our goal.

263

As stated in the introduction, each chapter residing within the covers of this volume stands on its own merits. If you wish, rip a chapter out of the book, and the chapter will still be a self-contained theory on that chapter's specific topic. However, the true purpose of this exercise is to blend the chapters into a holistic approach to management. There are certainly parts of the book that might seem almost brutal in their approach to human affairs. At other times, the book calls for forgiveness and leniency for the errors we all commit. That is the way it should be. There are situations in life when we need to stand on our values and say, enough is enough. Whether we realize it or not, we are in a real battle with real evil, so we must adopt a soldier's attitude. At other times, our warrior ways need to yield to our more gentle nature as we place human dignity and value above all else. To manage effectively and contribute to our bottom line, we need elements of both philosophies in our repertoire. Delineating one possible route for this destination is the ultimate goal of *Wingtips with Spurs*.

Whenever we witness an injustice or find evidence of discrimination, whenever we discover inequality or narrow-mindedness in our companies, it is our job—our primary duty—to put an immediate stop to these negative influences. It doesn't matter if you have a big title, a corner office, or a six-figure income. What matters is that you represent your chosen profession, management. When we fail to stand on the wall and protect our employers and employees from the enemies of integrity, decency, and the truth, then we have failed not only ourselves but also the profession as a whole. There is no one else in your organization who is more important to the defense of the company's virtues and values than its management individuals. I have heard it stated, "If not you, then who?"

As stated at the beginning of this journey, you are engaged in a sacred profession. Believing this statement is critical to your success at work and happiness in life. Others may be engaged in trivial matters; you are not. It doesn't matter whether you are just starting out in the management profession or whether you are battle-scared and road-weary; it is of the utmost importance that you are reminded everyday of the magnitude of your job and how valuable you are.

Last and most important: don't forget to give your Creator the glory for everything you accomplish.

Lesson from the Ranch

So strap on that belt buckle, pull on those boots and plop that cowboy hat on your head. Now you're ready. Giddy up!

Cowboy Wisdom

1. **ABSENTEEISM**... Nobody ever drowned in his own sweat.

2. **AFTER HOURS**......You're only young once. After that, you need some other excuse for acting like an idiot.

3. **AGE DISCRIMINATION**....When a cowboy is too old to set a bad example, he hands out good advice.

4. **ARGUING**....There's two theories to arguin' with a woman. Neither one works.

5. **BAD NEWS**....Unlike bad weather, bad news doesn't get better over the next few days.

6. **BIG PICTURE**....Boots, chaps, and cowboy hats ... nothing else matters.

7. **COMMUNICATION**....Never miss a good chance to shut up.

8. **CONFLICT**.......Speak your mind but ride a fast horse.

9. **CONSULTANTS**....Never ask a barber if he thinks you need a haircut.

10. **CREATIVITY**....Never, ever tell a cowboy how to do something. Tell 'em what you need, then watch how resourceful he can be.

11. **DECISIONS**....The chuck wagon's menu has two selections. Eat one of them or go hungry.

12. **DISABILITIES**....Life ain't about how fast you run or how high you climb, but how well you bounce.

13. **ETHICS**....Always do the right thing. This pacifies your family and keeps your enemies at bay.

14. **FADS — NO THANKS**.... Never try to train a bull to yodel. It fritters away your time and infuriates the bull.

15. **FIRING**....It doesn't take a genius to spot a goat in a flock of sheep.

16. **FUN AT WORK**....To ride or not to ride? What a stupid question!

17. **GOVERNMENT**....Tellin' the deputy to git lost and makin' 'em do it are two entirely different propositions.

18. **HIRING**....Never hire a man who wears gloves and smokes cigarettes. He'll spend way too much time pulling off his gloves and rolling cigarettes.

19. **LABOR RELATIONS**....When you're throwin' your weight around, be ready to have it thrown around by somebody else.

20. **LEADERSHIP**....If you're ridin' ahead of the herd, take a look back every now and then to make sure it's still there.

21. **MEETINGS**....If it don't seem like it's worth the effort, it probably ain't.

22. **MISSION STATEMENTS**....The best sermons are lived, not preached.

23. **MONEY**....The quickest way to double your money is to fold it over and put it back into your pocket.

24. **ORGANIZATIONAL CHARTS**....If you get to thinkin' you're a person of influence, try orderin' somebody else's dog around.

25. **PRIDE**....Don't swagger around the ranch in your Stetson and Tony Lamas when your wife has to work in town.

26. **RACIAL DISCRIMINATION**....A man is weighed by the bond of his word, the grit in his craw, and his love of God, Family, and Country. Nothing else carries weight.

27. **RUN, WHEN TO**....When your horse dies, get off.

28. **SAFETY**....Don't squat with your spurs on.

29. **SELF-IMPORTANCE** ....He thinks the sun came up just to hear him crow.

30. **SEXUAL HARASSMENT**....Always drink upstream from the herd.

31. **SPIRITUALITY**....Always travel with your pistol, jerky and Bible. These three things can getcha out of any tight spot.

32. **STANDING PLANS**....Don't interfere with something that ain't botherin' you none.

33. **STRATEGIC PLANNING**....Those who fail to plan, plan to fail.

34. **STRESS**....Forgive your enemies. It messes up their heads.

35. **SUCCESSION**....I can train a cowboy in a few weeks, but a good horse is hard to replace.

36. **TEAMWORK**....The strength of the ranch is the cowboy. The strength of the cowboy is the ranch.

37. **TRAINING**....Generally, you ain't learnin' nothing when your mouth's a-jawin'.

38. **TURNOVER**.......Only a dang fool will lose a good job, a good horse, or a good woman.

39. **VALUE**.......What price do you place on a crisp mountain morning?

40. **WORDS**....You can't unsay a cruel word.

41. **WRAPUP**....If you continue to ride off into the sunset, you'll ultimately wind up in the Pacific Ocean.

Sacred Words

1. **ABSENTEEISM**....A wise youth harvests in the summer, but one who sleeps during harvest is a disgrace. (Proverbs 10:5)

2. **AFTER HOURS**....Because we belong to the day, we must live decent lives for all to see. Don't participate in the darkness of wild parties and drunkenness, or in sexual promiscuity and immoral living, or in quarreling and jealousy. (Romans 13:13)

3. **AGE DISCRIMINATION**....And now, in my old age, don't set me aside. Don't abandon me when my strength is failing. (Psalm 71:9)

4. **ARGUING**....Don't pick a fight without reason, when no one has done you harm. (Proverbs 3:30)

5. **BAD NEWS**....Someone once told me, 'Saul is dead,' thinking he was bringing me good news. But I seized him and killed him at Ziklag. That's the reward I gave him for his news! (2 Samuel 4:10)

6. **BIG PICTURE**....But my life is worth nothing to me unless I use it for finishing the work assigned me by the Lord Jesus. (Acts 20:24)

7. **COMMUNICATION**....Wise words satisfy like a good meal; the right words bring satisfaction. (Proverbs 18:20)

8. **CONFLICT**....Then they began to argue among themselves about who would be the greatest among them. (Luke 22:24)

9. **CONSULTANTS**...Timely advice is lovely, like golden apples in a silver basket. (Proverbs 25:11)

10. **CREATIVITY**....It should be explained that all the Athenians as well as the foreigners in Athens seemed to spend all their time discussing the latest ideas. (Acts 17:21)

11. **DECISIONS**....The king speaks with divine wisdom; he must never judge unfairly. (Proverbs 16:10)

12. **DISABILITIES**....You have not taken care of the weak. You have not tended the sick or bound up the injured. You have not gone looking for those who have wandered away and are lost. Instead, you have ruled them with harshness and cruelty. (Ezekiel 34:4)

13. **ETHICS**....Don't be fooled by those who say such things, for "bad company corrupts good character. (1 Corinthians 15:33)

14. **FADS: NO THANKS**....History merely repeats itself. It has all been done before. Nothing under the sun is truly new. (Ecclesiastes 1:9)

15. **FIRING**....Even while we were with you, we gave you this command: 'Those unwilling to work will not get to eat.' (2 Thessalonians 3:10-12)

16. **FUN AT WORK**....A time to cry and a time to laugh. A time to grieve and a time to dance. (Ecclesiastes 3:4)

17. **GOVERNMENT**....They plan to topple me from my high position. They delight in telling lies about me. They praise me to my face but curse me in their hearts. (Psalms 62:4)

18. **HIRING**....Therefore, please command that cedars from Lebanon be cut for me. Let my men work alongside yours, and I will pay your men whatever wages you ask. As you know, there is no one among us who can cut timber like you Sidonians! (1 Kings 5:6)

19. **LABOR RELATIONS**....Can two people walk together without agreeing on the direction? (Amos 3:3)

20. **LEADERSHIP**....So ignore them. They are blind guides leading the blind, and if one blind person guides another, they will both fall into a ditch. (Matthew 15:14)

21. **MEETINGS**....On the first day of the week, we gathered with the local believers to share in the Lord's Supper. (Acts 20:7)

22. **MISSION STATEMENTS**....When people do not accept divine guidance, they run wild. But whoever obeys the law is joyful. (Proverbs 29:18)

23. **MONEY**....Those who love money will never
have enough. How meaningless to think that
wealth brings true happiness! (Ecclesiastes 5:10)

24. **ORGANIZATIONAL CHARTS**....No one can
serve two masters. For you will hate one and love
the other; you will be devoted to one and despise
the other. You cannot serve both God and
money. (Matthew 6:24)

25. **PRIDE**....Pride leads to disgrace, but with
humility comes wisdom. (Proverbs 11:2)

26. **RACIAL DISCRIMINATION**....There is no
longer Jew or Gentile, slave or free, male and
female. For you are all one in Christ Jesus.
(Galatians 3:28)

27. **RUN, WHEN TO**....Leave your simple ways
behind, and begin to live; learn to use good
judgment. (Proverbs 9:6)

28. **SAFETY**....If you want to live securely in the
land, follow my decrees and obey my regulations.
(Leviticus 25:18)

29. **SELF-IMPORTANCE**....Let someone else
praise you, not your own mouth — a stranger, not
your own lips. (Proverbs 27:2)

30. **SEXUAL HARASSMENT**....Can a man scoop
a flame into his lap and not have his clothes catch
on fire? (Proverb 6:27)

31. **SPIRITUALITY**....And what do you benefit if
you gain the whole world but are yourself lost or
destroyed? (Luke 9:25)

32. **STANDING PLANS**....Do to others as you
would like them to do to you. (Luke 6:31)

33. **STRATEGIC PLANNING**....Though good advice lies deep within the heart, a person with understanding will draw it out. (Proverbs 20:5)

34. **STRESS**....Don't worry about anything; instead, pray about everything. Tell God what you need, and thank him for all he has done. (Philippians 4:6)

35. **SUCCESSION**....But I tell you the truth; no prophet is accepted in his own hometown. (Luke 4:24)

36. **TEAMWORK**....Share each other's burdens, and in this way obey the law of Christ. If you think you are too important to help someone, you are only fooling yourself. You are not that important. (Galatians 6:2–3)

37. **TRAINING**....Instruct the wise and they will be even wiser. Teach the righteous, and they will learn even more. (Proverbs 9:9)

38. **TURNOVER**....The human spirit can endure a sick body, but who can bear a crushed spirit? (Proverbs 18:14)

39. **VALUE**....They are always thinking about how much it costs. 'Eat and drink,' they say, but they don't mean it. (Proverbs 23:7)

40. **WORDS**....Kind words are like honey— sweet to the soul and healthy for the body. (Proverbs 16:24)

41. **WRAP-UP**....The grace of the Lord Jesus be with you all. (Revelations 22:21)

APPENDIX C

Suggested Reading

Black Gun, Silver Star: The Life and Legend of Frontier Marshal Bass Reeves. Art T. Burton, University of Nebraska Press, 2006.

Blink: The Power of Thinking Without Thinking, Malcolm Gladwell, Little, Brown and Company, 2005.

Further Up the Organization, Robert Townsend, Knopf, 1984.

Freakonomics: A Rouge Economist Explores the Hidden Side of Everything, Steven D. Levitt, Stephen J. Dubner, William Morrow HarperCollins, 2005.

God and the New Physics, Paul Davies, Simon & Schuster, 1983.

Good to Great: Why Some Companies Make the Leap and Others Don't, Jim Collins, HarperCollins, 2001.

How to Argue and Win Every Time, Jerry Spence, St. Martin's Press, 1995.

Mere Christianity, C.S. Lewis, HarperCollins, 1952.

Negotiating a Labor Contract: A Management Handbook, Charles S. Loughran, BNA Books (Bureau of National Affairs), 2003.

Proving the Value of HR: How and Why to Measure ROI, Jack J. Phillips, Patricia Pulliam Phillips, Society for Human Management, 2005.

Sacred Hoops: Spiritual Lessons of a Hardwood Warrior, Phil Jackson, Hyperion Books, 1995.

The Conscious Universe: Parts and Wholes in Physical Reality, Menas Kafatos, Robert Nadeau, Springer-Verlag, 1990.

The Death of Common Sense: How Law is Suffocating America, Philip K Howard, Warner Books, 1996.

The Mind of God: The Scientific Basis for a Rational World, Paul Davies, Simon & Schuster, 1993.

The One Minute Manager: The Quickest Way to Increase Your Own Prosperity, Ken Blanchard, Spencer Johnson, William Morrow & Co, 1982.

About the Author

Michael L. Gooch, SPHR (Senior Professional in Human Resources) is the Corporate Regional Director of Human Resources for Pilgrim's Pride Corporation, the nation's largest chicken company and consistently recognized on Fortune's list of "America's Most Admired Companies". Prior to this, he worked in a variety of human resources positions at several locations for ConAgra Foods in Missouri and Arkansas. Mr. Gooch has also held managerial positions in Ladish Company, Armco Steel, RJR Nabisco / Del Monte USA, Tiffany Furniture and Prescolite. In his spare time, he has been an instructor in statistical process control at a community college. In addition to operating an independent consulting practice, Mr. Gooch previously held a consulting position with Traveler's Insurance.

Through the years, Mr. Gooch has won numerous eminent industry and governmental awards in leadership, teamwork and safety. Time not devoted to human resources management is spent on his 485 acre ranch raising Angus beef cattle.

Corporate Intelligence Awareness

Securing the Competitive Edge

By Rodger Nevill Harding

Corporate Intelligence Awareness: Securing the Competitive Edge

In this compelling new book by a former diplomat, you will learn the secrets (step by step) to developing an intelligence strategy by effective information gathering and analyzing, and then to delivering credible intelligence to senior management. Along the way, you will learn how to better read people and organizations and get them to open up and share information with you—all the while behaving in an ethical, legal manner. Understanding how intelligence is gathered and processed will keep you ahead of the game, protect your secrets, and secure your competitive edge!

ISBN: 1-895186-42-0 (hardcover)
ISBN: 1-895186-43-9 (PDF ebook)

Also available in other ebook formats. Order from your local bookseller, Amazon.com, or directly from the publisher at **http://www.mmpubs.com**

A New Book by Ida Shessel

MEETING with SUCCESS

Tips and Techniques for Great Meetings

Are People Finding Your Meetings Unproductive and Boring?

Turn ordinary discussions into focused, energetic sessions that produce positive results.

If you are a meeting leader or a participant who is looking for ways to get more out of every meeting you lead or attend, then this book is for you. It's filled with practical tips and techniques to help you improve your meetings.

You'll learn to spot the common problems and complaints that spell meeting disaster, how people who are game players can effect your meeting, fool-proof methods to motivate and inspire, and templates that show you how to achieve results. Learn to cope with annoying meeting situations, including problematic participants, and run focused, productive meetings.

ISBN: 1-897326-15-7   (paperback)

Also available in other ebook formats. Order from your local bookseller, Amazon.com, or directly from the publisher at **http://www.mmpubs.com**

Managing Smaller Projects

*Simply put, this book is about helping
people control smaller projects in a
logical and effective way, and making
the process run smoothly, and is
indeed a success in achieving that
goal.*

IEE Engineering Management (12/04)

Mike Watson
Award-winning trainer and PM Methodology guru

Managing Smaller Projects:
A Practical Approach

So called "small projects" can have potentially alarming consequences if they go wrong, but their control is often left to chance. The solution is to adapt tried and tested project management techniques.

This book provides a low overhead, highly practical way of looking after small projects. It covers all the essential skills: from project start-up, to managing risk, quality and change, through to controlling the project with a simple control system. It cuts through the jargon of project management and provides a framework that is as useful to those lacking formal training, as it is to those who are skilled project managers and want to control smaller projects without the burden of bureaucracy.

Read this best-selling book from the U.K., now making its North American debut. *IEE Engineering Management* praises the book, noting that "Simply put, this book is about helping people control smaller projects in a logical and effective way, and making the process run smoothly, and is indeed a success in achieving that goal."

Available in print format. Order from your local bookseller, Amazon.com, or directly from the publisher at **http:// www.mmpubs.com**

Managing
AGILE
PR JECTS
THE PROJECT MANAGEMENT ESSENTIALS LIBRARY

edited by
Kevin Aguanno
PMP, MAPM

Managing Agile Projects

Are you being asked to manage a project with unclear requirements, high levels of change, or a team using Extreme Programming or other Agile Methods?

If you are a project manager or team leader who is interested in learning the secrets of successfully controlling and delivering agile projects, then this is the book for you.

From learning how agile projects are different from traditional projects, to detailed guidance on a number of agile management techniques and how to introduce them onto your own projects, this book has the insider secrets from some of the industry experts – the visionaries who developed the agile methodologies in the first place.

ISBN: 1-895186-11-0   (paperback)
ISBN: 1-895186-12-9   (PDF ebook)

http://www.agilesecrets.com

101 Ways
New

To Reward
Team Members

For
$20
(or less!)

Kevin Aguanno

The Project Management Essentials Library

Your wallet is empty? And you still need to boost your team's performance?

Building team morale is difficult in these tough economic times. Author Kevin Aguanno helps you solve the team morale problem with ideas for team rewards that won't break the bank.

Learn over 100 ways you can reward your project team and individual team members for just a few dollars. Full of innovative (and cheap!) ideas. Even with the best reward ideas, rewards can fall flat if they are not suitable to the person, the organization, the situation, or the magnitude of the accomplishment. Learn the four key factors that will *maximize* the impact of your rewards, and *guarantee* delighted recipients.

101 Ways to Reward Team Members for $20 (or Less!) teaches you how to improve employee morale, improve employee motivation, improve departmental and cross-organizational teaming, maximize the benefits of your rewards and recognition programme, and avoid the common mistakes.

ISBN: 1-895186-04-8   (paperback)

Also available in ebook formats. Order from your local bookseller, Amazon.com, or directly from the publisher at **http://www.mmpubs.com**

Winston Churchill: The Agile Project Manager

Today's pace of change has reached unprecedented levels only seen in times of war. As a result, project management has changed accordingly with the pressure to deliver and make things count quickly. This recording looks back at a period of incredible change and mines lessons for Project Managers today.

In May 1940, the United Kingdom (UK) was facing a dire situation, an imminent invasion. As the evacuation of Dunkirk unfolded, the scale of the disaster became apparent. The army abandoned 90% of its equipment, the RAF fighter losses were deplorable, and over 200 ships were lost.

Winston Churchill, one of the greatest leaders of the 20th century, was swept into power. With depleted forces and no organized defense, the situation required a near miracle. Churchill had to mobilize quickly and act with agility to assemble a defense. He had to make the right investment choices, deploy resources, and deliver a complete project in a fraction of the time. This recording looks at Churchill as an agile Project Manger, turning a disastrous situation into an unexpected victory.

ISBN: 1-895186-50-1   (Audio CD)
ISBN: 1-897326-38-6   (DVD)

Order from your local bookseller, Amazon.com, or directly from the publisher at **http://www.mmpubs.com**

Churchill's Adaptive Enterprise: Lessons for Business Today

This book analyzes a period of time from World War II when Winston Churchill, one of history's most famous leaders, faced near defeat for the British in the face of sustained German attacks. The book describes the strategies he used to overcome incredible odds and turn the tide on the impending invasion. The historical analysis is done through a modern business and information technology lens, describing Churchill's actions and strategy using modern business tools and techniques. Aimed at business executives, IT managers, and project managers, the book extracts learnings from Churchill's experiences that can be applied to business problems today. Particular themes in the book are knowledge management, information portals, adaptive enterprises, and organizational agility.

Eric Hoffer Book Award (2007) Winner

ISBN: 1-895186-19-6   (paperback)
ISBN: 1-895186-20-X   (PDF ebook)

Order from your local bookseller, Amazon.com, or directly from the publisher at **http://www.mmpubs.com/churchill**

By Peter R. Garber

Want to Get Ahead in Your Career?

Do you find yourself challenged by office politics, bad things happen-ing to good careers, dealing with the "big cheeses" at work, the need for effective networking skills, and keeping good working relation-ships with coworkers and bosses? *Winning the Rat Race at Work* is a unique book that provides you with case studies, interactive exercises, self-assessments, strategies, evaluations, and models for overcom-ing these workplace challenges. The book illustrates the stages of a career and the career choices that determine your future, empowering you to make positive changes.

Written by Peter R. Garber, the author of *100 Ways to Get on the Wrong Side of Your Boss*, this book is a must read for anyone interested in getting ahead in his or her career. You will want to keep a copy in your top desk drawer for ready reference whenever you find yourself in a challenging predica-ment at work.

ISBN: 1-895186-68-4 (paperback)

Also available in ebook formats. Order from your local bookseller, Amazon.com, or directly from the publisher at **http://www.mmpubs.com/rats**

100 Ways to Get on the Wrong Side of your Boss

And Strategies to Prevent you from Getting There!

Author of Winning the Rat Race at Work

Need More Help with the Politics at Work?

100 Ways To Get On The Wrong Side Of Your Boss (And Strategies to Prevent You from Getting There!) was written for anyone who has ever been frustrated by his or her working relationship with the boss—and who hasn't ever felt this way! Bosses play a critically important role in your career success and getting on the wrong side of this important individual in your working life is not a good thing.

Each of these 100 Ways is designed to illustrate a particular problem that you may encounter when dealing with your boss and then an effective strategy to prevent this problem from reoccurring. You will learn how to deal more effectively with your boss in this fun and practical book filled with invaluable advice that can be utilized every day at work.

Written by Peter R. Garber, the author of *Winning the Rat Race at Work*, this book is a must read for anyone interested in getting ahead. You will want to keep a copy in your top desk drawer for ready reference whenever you find yourself in a challenging predicament at work.

ISBN: 1-895186-98-6   (paperback)

Order from your local bookseller, Amazon.com, or directly from the publisher at **http://www.InTroubleAtWork.com**

The Elusive Lean Enterprise

In today's fast-paced and volatile business environment, customers are demanding increased flexibility and lower cost, and companies must operate in a waste-free environment to maintain a competitive edge and grow margins. Lean Enterprise is the process that companies are adopting to provide superior customer service and improve bottom line performance.

Are you contemplating Lean Enterprise for your manufacturing or office facility? Are you already implementing Lean, but dissatisfied with the speed of change? Do your employees think that Lean is just the new flavor of the month? Are you being forced to go Lean by your customers?

This book is designed to help guide you through the Lean transformation and avoid the pitfalls. Find out why many companies are failing to live up to the promise of Lean, and why there may be alternatives to outsourcing or going offshore.

ISBN: 1-897326-64-5   (paperback)

Order from your local bookseller, Amazon.com, or directly from the publisher at **http://www.mmpubs.com**

 **The Project Management
Audio Library**

In a recent CEO survey, the leaders of today's largest corporations identified project management as the top skillset for tomorrow's leaders. In fact, many organizations place their top performers in project management roles to groom them for senior management positions. Project managers represent some of the busiest people around. They are the ones responsible for planning, executing, and controlling most major new business activities.

Expanding upon the successful *Project Management Essentials Library* series of print and electronic books, Multi-Media Publications has launched a new imprint called the *Project Management Audio Library*. Under this new imprint, MMP is publishing audiobooks and recorded seminars focused on professionals who manage individual projects, portfolios of projects, and strategic programmes. The series covers topics including agile project management, risk management, project closeout, interpersonal skills, and other related project management knowledge areas.

This is not going to be just the "same old stuff" on the critical path method, earned value, and resource levelling; rather, the series will have the latest tips and techniques from those who are at the cutting edge of project management research and real-world application.

www.PM-Audiobooks.com

Printed in the United States
122632LV00001B/45/P